'Professor Bowker has written a book of penetrating insight, highlighting the importance of religions in the contemporary world as forces for both harm and good, and the necessity of both explaining and understanding them.'
Gavin Flood, FBA, Professor of Hindu Studies and Comparative Religion, University of Oxford

'Don't be fooled by the ease of reading *Religion Hurts*, its seeming lightness of touch. Bowker's insight is as penetrating as it comes, the distillation of decades of scholarly study.'
Damian Howard, SJ, Provincial of the Jesuits in Britain

'This is a fine work. Its rich array of literary illustrations and detailed affirmation of scientific knowledge will surely inspire new thinking about the nature of religious belief and its role in human affairs. It is particularly impressive in its insight into Islamic culture and intra-Islamic conflict, and it shows something of the fresh understanding needed for constructive Christian–Islamic engagement.'
Peter Barrett, Senior Research Associate, School of Religion, Philosophy and Classics, and formerly Associate Professor of Physics, University of KwaZulu-Natal, South Africa

'Bowker draws on a cross-civilizational knowledge of religion, philosophy and science to explore key questions confronting the world: what are religions, why are they involved in so much harm as well as good, and how can we learn to live with differences of world view? A work of deep understanding, humanity and insight to help counter the division and conflict of our times.'
Quinton Deeley, Senior Lecturer in Social Behaviour and Neurodevelopment, Institute of Psychiatry, Psychology and Neuroscience, Kings College, London

'John Bowker is a master blender of religious anthropologies, ethics, history, philosophy, the tussle between reason and emotion – all overlain by sensitivity and humanity. All his gifts are on display in this absorbing book.'
Peter Hennessy FBA, Attlee Professor of Contemporary British History, Queen Mary University of London

'Written by a world leader in inter-religious understanding, this is a perfect book for Christians, Muslims and those of other faiths who want to find better solutions for living together in our modern world. It will also encourage a better understanding of the motivations behind the choices made by people of faith, which can hurt others.'
Darryl Macer, President, American University of Sovereign Nations, and former UNESCO Regional Advisor for Asia and the Pacific

'This is vintage Bowker: reviewing a vast religious terrain – lit by philosophy, anthropology, genetics, neuroscience and, of course, poetry – he offers penetrating insights into conflict, altruism and "humanity" itself.'
Eleanor Nesbitt, Professor Emeritus, Warwick Religions and Education Research Unit, University of Warwick

'Drawing together philosophy, theology, religious studies and the latest neuroscience into a new synthesis, Bowker shows why religion remains an important part of every culture. This brilliant and perceptive book helps us to see clearly why it is important to understand religion, and how to cope wisely with its impact in the twenty-first century.'
Mark Williams, Emeritus Professor of Clinical Psychology, University of Oxford

John Bowker is Emeritus Professor at Gresham College, London. He has been Professor or Adjunct Professor of Religious Studies at the universities of Cambridge, Lancaster and Pennsylvania, and at North Carolina State University. He has been a consultant for UNESCO, as well as a BBC broadcaster. He is the author or editor of more than 40 books, including *The Oxford Dictionary of World Religions* (Oxford University Press, 1997), *Is God a Virus? Genes, Culture and Religion* (SPCK, 1995), *The Meanings of Death* (Cambridge University Press, 2008, winner of the HarperCollins Prize), *What Muslims Believe* (Oneworld, 2009), *God: A Very Short Introduction* (Oxford University Press, 2014), *Beliefs that Changed the World* (Quercus, 2015) and *Why Religions Matter* (Cambridge University Press, 2015).

Religion
Hurts
Why religions
do harm
as well
as good

John Bowker

spck

First published in Great Britain in 2018

Society for Promoting Christian Knowledge
36 Causton Street
London SW1P 4ST
www.spck.org.uk

British Library Cataloguing-in-Publication Data
A catalogue record for this book is available from the British Library

ISBN 978–0–281–08016–8
eBook ISBN 978–0–281–07690–1

Typeset by Manila Typesetting Company
First printed in Great Britain by TJ International
Subsequently digitally reprinted in Great Britain

eBook by Manila Typesetting Company

Produced on paper from sustainable forests

Contents

Acknowledgements

My thanks go to many people who have made this book possible, but above all to Margaret, my wife. We have written this book together, and I offer it to her now with deepest gratitude and love. Mona and Quinton Deeley have given constant help and encouragement, partly by their criticisms and suggestions of reading, but much more with their insights and ideas. Chip Coakley checked and completed references and quotations when I could no longer physically do so myself. For the same reason, Peter Girling of Cambridge University Library gave indispensable help with the new catalogue, as also did Mike Lumsden with my computer: thank you both. And thanks also to Sarah Brunning for unfailing and constant support. At SPCK, Philip Law has been a brilliant editor, taking immense trouble with the many disruptions, particularly of timetables, brought about by my changes of health. It has been a pleasure to work together. I am grateful also to Rima Devereaux and the editorial and production teams. The book might still not have appeared had it not been for the exemplary work of the copy-editor, Mollie Barker: her skills and eye for detail were breathtaking, and I am grateful to her for being so patient with me. A final word of thanks goes to Dr Amanda Cox whose unstinting care made the completion of this book possible.

A note on references and transliteration

A book about religions draws inevitably on a wide range of different topics, and as a result many books and articles have been quoted or mentioned. The details about them are given, not in footnotes, but in the Bibliography. References will be found under the name of the author or title, with the page number where applicable.

In this book the transliteration of other languages is not precise. It does not always include diacritical marks. Thus 'Umar appears as Umar. There is a particular problem in Arabic. The Arabic word for 'the' is *al*, and it is attached to its noun. Thus 'the house' is in Arabic *albait*. A widespread convention in transliterating Arabic inserts a hyphen between *al* and the following noun, hence *al-bait*. That, however, is unhelpful and misleading because it obliterates the distinction between two different groups of letters in the Arabic alphabet, the 14 so-called 'sun letters' (in contrast to the 'moon letters') where the letter *l* of *al* merges with the first letter of the noun. Thus 'the sun' is *ashshams*, not *alshams*. Authors who know Arabic respect this, but it creates problems in the alphabetical order of an Index. I have therefore adopted a compromise between the unhelpful convention and the proper respect for Arabic: for the 'sun letters' I have inserted a hyphen between the article and the noun (e.g. *al-shams*), and for the 'moon letters' I have followed Arabic usage and attached the article to the noun (e.g. *alQur'an*). So, for example, the following terms appear in the book: *alkifayah* and al-Salaf al-Salihin.

Introduction

This is a short book. It was meant to be even shorter. I was asked to write a brief pamphlet (one in a series) to answer the questions, 'Why are there different religions? Do the differences make a difference?' At first sight, that may seem a bit dull, rather like asking, 'Why are there pebbles on a beach?'

In fact, if you look more closely, those questions are challenging and by no means simple – and the question about the *differences* between religions turns out to be extremely urgent as well. In 2017, there were horrific attacks in the UK (three in three months in Manchester and London) made by people who had some connection with Islam. It made inevitable the question asked by many people as to whether religions do more harm than good. In the context of terror attacks, it is often asked in the form, 'Why are there different religions, and why are they so often fighting each other and killing us?'

We may want to challenge the way in which that question is put, but with religions involved around the world in so many conflicts and acts of aggression (some might say 'terrorism'), it's easy to see why it is being asked. And unless we can answer it, we have no chance of building successfully the multicultural societies that are now an ambition and increasingly a commonplace in the modern world.

But when we get down to it, we find that the question is extremely difficult. One immediate complication is that when people try to answer it, either in general or in relation to a particular incident, they frequently give totally contradictory answers.

Thus when in Manchester, in May 2017, a suicide bomber with unequivocal Muslim connections killed 22 people in addition to himself and injured more than 200 others, many Muslims said that it was the act of a deranged individual and that it had nothing to do with the real Islam: Islam, they said, is a truly peace-loving religion. Many non-Muslims agreed, including Jeremy Corbyn, the leader of the UK Labour Party, who said repeatedly in his election campaign at the time that the act was 'a perversion of Islam, a complete perversion of Islam'.

Yet there are other Muslims who take the opposite point of view and who insist that the *truly* faithful are those who obey the command of God in the Qur'an to fight against, and if necessary kill, those who attack any Muslims. It is an obligation on able-bodied young men to do so. That is why these other Muslims see so many around the world as enemies and as legitimate targets because of their attacks on Muslim countries. From this point of view, Salman Abedi, the suicide bomber in Manchester, was 'a true Muslim', a martyr whose place is now in alJanna, the Garden (of Paradise). Martyrs are defined as 'those who die in the cause of God', and if possible they are buried in the clothes they were wearing when they died so that they will be recognized at once in the Hereafter (*alAkhira*) as martyrs.

Which – if either – of those two accounts of Islam is correct? Or are both? Clearly, the answer we give makes a massive difference, but no serious response is possible unless we understand the long-running, complicated and often fiercely contested arguments *among Muslims themselves.*

Central is the issue of Jihad. Jihad (from *jahada*, 'he struggled') is often translated as War, or Holy War, but in the Qur'an there are two kinds of Jihad (struggle on behalf of God), the Greater and the Lesser. When Muhammad and his troops were returning to Medina from fighting a battle, he told them that they were returning from the Lesser Jihad to the Greater Jihad: they were returning to the effort that all must make to live as God commands, and that is the Greater Jihad.

Nevertheless, the Lesser Jihad may include fighting and killing. It is an obligation on Muslims as a whole, *fard alkifayah* in contrast to *fard alayn* which are personal and individual obligations: Jihad is then obligatory only for Muslim men who are sane, who have reached the age of puberty, and who can support their family while they are thus engaged (see Doi, pp. 441–4). The obligation arises whenever fellow-Muslims are attacked, as is now the case in many places around the world:

> Permission [to fight] is given to those against whom war is made, because they are wronged – and truly Allah is most powerful for their aid – [they are] those who have been expelled from their homes in defiance of right – [for no cause] except that they say, 'Our Lord is Allah.'
>
> (Qur'an 22.39)

There is, therefore, direct authority from the Qur'an to engage in defensive war and killing. There are, however, extremely clear rules governing Jihad in the Qur'an, in instructions from Muhammad, and in rules of the second Caliph, Umar. For example, it is forbidden 'to touch the old, those close to death, women, children, and infants'. Umar added that neither trees nor flocks should be damaged, unless while getting food for the army. There are clear limits (*hudud*) in Qur'an and Tradition on what can be done in the Lesser Jihad. Many Muslims, therefore, argue that some things done in recent years to defend Islam (especially indiscriminate killings, as with vehicles, knives and bombs) are actually forbidden, and that those who do such things cannot be true Muslims. That is why, after the attack in Manchester, several imams refused to conduct the funeral rites for Abedi because he was no longer, in their view, a true Muslim.

What is obvious in that brief summary is the fact that *both* sides in this disputed understanding of Islam believe that they are the truly faithful Muslims. Both of those contradictory accounts draw on the same sources of Qur'an, Hadith (authoritative traditions) and Sharia to justify their arguments. There are deep divisions within Islam, just as there are in other religions. So even from that one example we can see how complicated the issues are going to be when we try to understand why there are differences between and within religions, and why religions are involved in conflicts or acts of aggression.

That is why what might have been a short pamphlet has become a longer book. There are formidable difficulties involved when we try to answer the questions: why have the differences arisen between Islam and other religions, and among Muslims themselves? Why have there been equally divisive differences between and within other religions? And do the differences make a serious difference? Or can we find ways in which to acknowledge them but not to allow them to destroy our attempt to live together in tolerant multicultural, multifaith communities?

Those are not easy questions to answer, and as we attempt to do so, we will find that one thing most definitely leads to another. Like the wide-flowing delta of a river, one part of an answer spreads out and divides into many additional questions. The issues involved in understanding religions are not simple, and there are two immediate areas of complexity.

First, it is impossible to say why there are so many religions without knowing in the first place what religions are. Some people at the present time, as we will see, argue that there is no such thing as 'religion': 'religion', they claim, is a nineteenth-century category imposed by European colonialists on different cultures and civilizations in order to bring them under control. 'There is consensus', as Michael Bergunder has put it recently (p. 41), 'that the modern concept of religion derived from a *historical* European prototype.' What the word *religio* meant for Lucretius when he wrote the line (*De Rerum Natura*, 1.101) 'Tantum religio potuit suadere malorum' ('How many evils has religion caused!') is very different from what Marx and Engels observed in Europe which led Marx to describe 'religion' as the opiate of the people.

It follows, second, that we have to ask why we use the word 'religion' at all. What are the beliefs and behaviours that have evoked a specific word to describe them? We cannot answer that question without asking what part the beliefs and behaviours that we call 'religious' have played in human evolution and history. Religions are universal and they have created many different forms of civilization and society – as they still do in many places.

This book, therefore, has to recognize how fundamental those two connected questions are: what has led us to use the word 'religion'? And what part have religions played in evolution and human history? Only then can we begin to see why there are so many different, often competing, beliefs, and why they have taken such varied forms of organization and structure.

But do the differences make such a difference that religions are inevitably drawn into competition and conflict with each other? Or are the many *apparent* differences between religions simply variations on the theme of human nature – different accounts of what it means to be human? It is that issue which has now become so urgent. Yes, religions often live peacefully together, and certainly they have created and sustained spectacular and often enduring cultures and civilizations; they have given meaning, purpose and vision to innumerable lives. At the same time, however, religions have been and still are involved in many of the most difficult and apparently insoluble conflicts around the world.

None of this is new. More than 30 years ago, on Monday, 13 May 1985, a whole page of *The Guardian* was devoted to 'Overseas News'. There were 12 stories on the page, and all but one were stories of violent behaviours or episodes: 'Sri Lanka Killings "Revenge"'; 'Six Shot Dead in Bangladesh Protests over Koran Suit'; 'Cry Rings Out to Kill Extremists'; 'Death Toll of India Terror Bomb Reaches 80'; 'Explosion in Teheran Kills 15', to mention only a few. Of those 11 stories of violence all but one had clear religious contributions to them.

Since that time, the involvement of religions in conflict, violence and terrorism has not diminished. It has literally 'come closer to home' with the rise of groups like alQaeda, the Taliban and Da'ish, and with attacks on people in major cities. At the time of writing, the civil wars in Syria and Yemen have continued with renewed ferocity; in Uttar Pradesh the newly appointed First Minister was reported to have said that for every Hindu killed by a Muslim, a hundred Muslims will be killed in return; in Myanmar Aung San Suu Kyi had to deny that the treatment by the majority (mainly Buddhist) of the minority (Muslim) Rohingya amounted to ethnic cleansing; in two Egyptian cities, Alexandria and Cairo, Coptic Christians were killed in their churches on Palm Sunday; in Chechnya it was reported that State attacks on gay people drew on support from the Muslim condemnation of homosexuality.

Moving from *The Guardian* of 1985 to *The Times* of 10 May 2017 (the day on which these words are being written), we find nine stories which have 'clear religious contributions to them'. For example: 'New Islamist Video Shows Beheading of Russian "spy"'; 'Renegade Bishop Raises Threat of Schism over Gays'; 'Creeping Islamism Is Undermining Indonesian Democracy'; 'Jewish Shop Threatened by Man with a Meat Cleaver' (the man was heard shouting, 'You Jews run away from here before I kill you'); 'Hardline Muslims Cheer Jailing of Jakarta's Christian Governor'.

It is not the case that religions are the sole cause of those events, nor is it the case that the definition of 'terrorism' is non-controversial. But the opposite claim is also false – that violence of this kind is not caused by religions but only by the perversion and corruption of religions. Deeply rooted and authoritative religious beliefs can be among the many reasons why such things happen. There is an important truth in a cartoon published in the *Daily Telegraph* (to which I drew attention at the beginning of *Why Religions*

Matter) which depicted the feet of victims in a morgue with the tags of identity attached to them. But instead of the names of the people being written on the tags, the causes of their death were written instead: 'Killed by religious bigots, Bosnia'; 'Killed by religious bigots, N. Ireland'; 'Killed by religious bigots, India'; 'Killed by religious bigots, Iraq'; 'Killed by religious bigots, Azerbaijan'; 'Killed by religious bigots, Auschwitz'; 'Killed by religious bigots, Beirut'; 'Killed by religious bigots, Armenia'.

It is clear, therefore, that religions, in their beliefs, behaviours and institutions, are involved in much that is harmful. But at the same time they are involved in much that is extremely good. That is exactly what I have called elsewhere 'the paradox of religions': religions are such bad news (when they are) only because they are such good news. They give order, meaning and purpose to human life, but they also give rise to despotic control in social organization and to intolerance in individual lives. Religions are so profoundly important to so many people that when they are threatened, there will always be some to defend them.

And that explains the title of this book. Religion hurts. It does so, *both* because it causes damage (in many senses) *and also* because it is costly and painful to its adherents when it is lived to the full: it can then become demanding and precious beyond price. Mother Teresa is a familiar and obvious example of how costly in personal terms that can be, as also is Dietrich Bonhoeffer who was executed in 1945 for his resistance to the Nazi regime. In 1937, when the rise of the Nazis seemed unstoppable, he wrote his account of what it means to be a Christian, calling it *Nachtfolge*. When it was translated into English, it was given the supremely appropriate title *The Cost of Discipleship*.

The point to be emphasized is that *both sides* of the paradox of religions belong together – a point graphically underlined by a worldwide survey in 2017 of people's attitudes to religions: in response to the question 'Do you think that religions do more harm than good, or do you think that religions do more good than harm?' the answers were almost equally divided. We need to understand why, *paradoxically*, both can be true. Aspects of religious beliefs and behaviours are surely open to criticism and protest, but at the same time, for the vast majority of people, their religion is the familiar place where they belong and for which they are grateful. As a Christian Thanksgiving puts it, 'We give thanks for our creation, preservation, and all the blessings of this life, . . . for the means of grace and for the hope of glory.'

Those very different outcomes create the paradox of religion, that religions are such bad news (when they are) because they are such good news. If religions did not matter so much to so many people, they might well have disappeared long ago. But they do matter and they are still very much with us. And that is why those questions about religions (why are there so many different religions? do the differences make a difference?) need so urgently to be addressed and answered. Back in 1985, I made this appeal:

> The entanglement of religions in virtually all the intransigent problems which confront and threaten us means that we must become more serious in the ways in which we try to understand the power of religious belief both for evil and for good . . . One of the most obvious reasons why we seem to drift from one disastrous ineptitude to another is, ironically, that far too few politicians have read Religious Studies at a University. As a result, they literally do not

know what they are talking about on almost any of the major international issues. They simply cannot. It is time we began to educate ourselves, not just in economics, or in politics, or in technology, but also in the dynamics of religious belief and continuity, because whether we like it or not, it is religion which still matters more than anything else to most people alive today.

The appeal was unavailing then, so it may seem pointless to try again now. But we live in extremely dangerous times, and the weapons available to those in conflict are now a great deal more sophisticated than the swords and spears of old. As Samuel Johnson put it, 'War has means of destruction more formidable than the cannon and the sword' – and he wrote that nearly 250 years ago when he was protesting against a possible Falklands War! We live now in a world where 'the means of destruction' are much more formidable, including, as they do, nuclear, chemical, biological and cybernetic weapons. Some of these have already been used in conflicts involving religions. For that reason alone we need to understand what religions are, and what part they play in human life and history.

Additional texts

In trying to keep this book as brief as possible, I have drawn attention to some major issues without being able to explore them further in any detail. To have done so would have been to disrupt completely the narrative of the book. There are, however, sections of additional text: they draw on an article and a book written some time ago, but they have been extensively rewritten and revised for this book.

The first of the major issues is raised in the Introduction to this book which begins with the Manchester and London attacks in 2017 and with Muslim arguments about Jihad. It raises sharp questions about how Muslims and non-Muslims can live together. Additional text 1 looks at the importance of treaties in Islam in understanding the relationship between Muslims and non-Muslims. It suggests how the so-called Domain of Peace (Dar al-Sulh) might be developed further in the modern world, taking as an example the way in which that might be applied to the currently tense issue of whether women should or should not wear the *niqab* or the *burqa*.

Another of the major issues between religions (taken further in Additional text 2) asks whether they are united or divided in their understandings of God. The claim, putting it as briefly as possible, is this: if 'God' transcends by definition all that humans can say or think about God, then God (whatever God is) is the ultimate truth and concern of all (theistic) religions even though their accounts of the nature and character of 'God' (the aseity of God, what God is *a se*) are extremely different. The argument might then be that 'God' is the word people use when they want to talk about whatever is the ultimate and absolute Reality. But, as I have shown in my *God: A Very Short Introduction* (p. 16), religions identify and describe the ultimately Real in different ways, leading to divergent and deeply divisive characterizations of God. Even so, one can still say that they are at least at one in believing that there is such Reality 'in its infinite mystery beyond the scope of the human intellect'. If that is so, then one might conclude that religions are simply different roads leading to the same destination. But not all roads lead to the same destination simply by virtue of being roads. So do those differences make a difference in terms of ultimate destination or truth? Or might one of those accounts be true to the exclusion of others?

Another major issue that arises when we are trying to understand why there are so many different religions, and when we ask the question as to whether those differences make a difference, lies in the fact that most religions rely on texts and teachers that have great authority. But those texts and teachings have to be interpreted, and there is no agreement within or between religions on what kinds of interpretation are legitimate or recognized as acceptable. As a result, there can be deeply divergent interpretations of texts and teachings which often create irreconcilable differences within religions. It is the issue of what is known as 'hermeneutics', and it is explored further in Chapter 4 and in Additional text 3.

1

Religion and religions

'Why are there so many different religions?' It seems at first sight a fairly straightforward question. It turns out, though, to be complicated. A first complication is that we need to know what religions are before we can see in what ways, if any, they are different – and 'different', not just from each other, but also from other human activities. We are told, for example, that some people make a religion out of their support for a football team. There has been a long debate about whether other belief-systems, such as Marxism or even humanism, are religions. A few years ago, after a disastrous fire in a store in Manchester, a spokesman said: 'There was no sprinkler system. That depends on a Local Authority's requirements and they do vary. We comply with them religiously, but in this case there was no such requirement.'

So what do the words 'religion' and 'religiously' actually mean? Can we define the word 'religion' so as to make it clear what we're looking at when we ask why there are so many different religions?

And that's the problem. We all know more or less what religions are, but if we are asked to define the word 'religion' more exactly (so that it comprehensively includes some things and excludes others), we find that it is difficult, even impossible, to do so. The words 'religion' and 'religious' cover such a vast multitude of beliefs and practices, of organizations and structures, of every kind of human behaviour, that we cannot pack everything into a definition that includes it all. At the beginning of *The Oxford Dictionary of World Religions* I wrote that this resembles the dilemma that faced Augustine over 'time':

> A strange thing about religion is that we all know what it is until someone asks us to tell them. As Augustine said of time: 'What, then, is time? If no one asks me I know; but if I have to say what it is to someone who asks, I know not.'

It was one of the many enduring achievements of the philosopher Wittgenstein to warn us against the danger of thinking that words or nouns like 'religion' have a single, definable meaning, or that they are pointing to a single thing or essence. In other words, he was advising us to curb our craving for generality, our tendency to look for something in common in all the entities which we describe under a general term.

The example he took was 'games'. That word is often used as though there are features common to all games (for example, competition or rules) from which a definition of the word 'games' can be derived. Against this, Wittgenstein argued that what games have in common are not single, universal properties, but many resemblances that characterize certain very diverse activities as 'games'. He called those resemblances 'family resemblances'. In *Philosophical Investigations* 66–7 he wrote:

> Consider for example the proceedings that we call 'games'. I mean board-games, card-games, ball-games, Olympic Games, and so on. What is common to them all? – Don't say: 'There *must* be something in common, or they would not be called "games"' – but *look and see* whether there is

14

anything common to all. For if you look at them you will not see something that is common to *all* but similarities, relationships, and a whole series of them at that. To repeat: don't think, but look! ...

And the result of this examination is: we see a complicated network of similarities overlapping and criss-crossing: sometimes overall similarities, sometimes similarities of detail.

I can think of no better expression to characterise these similarities than 'family resemblances'; for the various resemblances between the members of a family: build, features, colour of eyes, gait, temperament, etc. etc. overlap and criss-cross in the same way. And I shall say: 'games' form a family.

In a similar way, we can say that 'religions' form a family with many resemblances, but without the same essence or identity. Any candidate to be considered 'a religion' or 'a game' must have some of the family resemblances even though no religion or game has them all.

Making a decision about what counts is not easy. In the case of games, for example, the International Olympic Committee meets at regular intervals to decide which games or sports will be admitted to the Olympic Games. On 3 August 2016, baseball and softball, karate, sport climbing, skateboarding and surfing were all admitted to the Tokyo games of 2020. If we go back a hundred years to 1912 (there were no Games during the First World War), the sports included tug-of-war and sculpture, and games aspiring to become part of the Olympics were demonstrated, including Pärk and bicycle polo. Chess and bridge applied for 2020 – but are they sports or games? In 2017, the European Court of Justice decided that bridge is not a sport and therefore cannot claim the exemption from VAT on tournament entry fees that is allowed to sports or games. Shifting to religions, is Scientology a religion or is it a philosophy? Does it have charitable status (with the tax benefits that that would bring) or not?

In trying, therefore, to answer the question, 'Why are there different religions?', we have to recognize from the outset that there is no single 'thing' of which religions are different examples. We will find many family resemblances but also much divergence and variety, even when they seem to be doing 'the same thing'. In *World Religions* (p. 6), I gave some examples of that combination of 'resemblance and divergence' when I tried to indicate an answer to the question, 'What does it mean to be religious?'

> It means so many things to so many different people that often they contradict each other. It can mean believing that God is the source and the goal of life, or that this is at best a juvenile distraction; it can mean loving one's neighbour as oneself, or excommunicating him or her to a fate far worse than death; it can mean consulting witches for wisdom, or burning them alive; having a soul, or not having a soul; obeying the command to be fruitful, or taking a lifelong vow to be celibate; withdrawing into silence, or speaking in tongues; it can require shaving one's head, or never cutting one's hair; it can involve some people going to mosque on Friday, others to synagogue on Saturday, others to church on Sunday; it can mean praying, meditating, levitating, worshipping, entering into trance and ecstasy; it can mean building St Paul's Cathedral, or the Golden Temple, or the Great Pyramid; it can send people across oceans and continents to go on pilgrimage to holy places, or to convert others, or to fight Crusades, holy wars, or Jihads; it has also

meant the inspired creation of music, art, icons, symbols, poetry at the very farthest stretch of human imagination, and yet it can also reveal itself as trivial sentiment.

There are of course many who believe that religion *can* be defined with such precision that it will identify one and only one religion as true. Other religions will contain some elements of that truth (hence 'family resemblances'), but, so the claim goes, only one will contain them all. This is how John Henry Newman (1801–91) put it (vol. V, p. 194):

All religions, the various heathen religions as well as the Mosaic religion, have many things in them which are very much the same. They seem to come from one common origin, and so far have the traces of truth upon them . . . the difference between them being that the heathen religions are a true religion corrupted; the Jewish, a true religion dead; and Christianity the true religion living and perfect.

Newman stated in 1879 that he had spent 50 years 'resisting to the best of my powers the spirit of Liberalism in religion' ('Biglietto Speech'; cf. Ward, *Life*, II):

Liberalism in religion is the doctrine that there is no positive truth in religion, but that one creed is as good as another, and this is the teaching which is gaining substance and force daily. It is inconsistent with the recognition of any religion as true.

To the question, therefore, *Is One Religion as Good as Another?* (the title of a book written in 1887 by J. MacLaughlin, one of Newman's followers), the unequivocal answer is no: the only true religion is the one in which there is unerring authority and an infallible voice – not even in Christianity, but only in the Catholic Church.

Here, the problems of definition become obvious. That argument depends on an agreement that the two characteristics of inerrancy and infallibility define what true religion is. But other religions (for example, Islam) make comparable claims to inerrancy and infallibility, and yet in those religions there are beliefs that are incompatible and contradictory of each other: they cannot all be true.

Even more fundamentally, the argument depends also on the definition of the word 'good'. Good for what? holiness? salvation? enlightenment? rebirth? nirvana? the love of God and of one's neighbour? It is like saying that we all have to eat, but only one diet is good: good for what? health? slimming? vitamins? enjoyment? building up stamina for a marathon?

Wittgenstein's warning about finding a single definition for immense complexity is the first difficulty in trying to know why there are different religions. There is then an even deeper problem. There are many who argue that there is no such 'thing' as religion at all. In common with many nouns, the word 'religion' is not pointing to a single, identifiable essence (for example, a concern with ultimate reality or with transcendence or with 'the good life') which we might then find exemplified in different religions. In their view, 'religion' is an academic category with its own history in European thought which has been imposed on human behaviours around the world. Those behaviours are so extremely diverse that they cannot be corralled into a single category.

Indeed, the argument is sometimes extended to claim that the imposition of the category of 'religion' is a continuation of colonial imperialism. It brings everything from aborigines to Asia under the control of a European category of explanation. Many foreign words are translated into English as 'religion', but in their own indigenous context and history they have their own highly specific meaning and use. Think, for example, of *din* in Islam, *dharma* in India, *zongjiao* in China, *shukyo* in Japan. To translate those words as 'religion' is to impose an alien category. Instead, so the argument goes, we should start from the behaviours (both individual and social) as and where they occur, and allow the explanation of what they are to arise from within their own categories and subject matter.

So the question, 'Why are there different religions?', is certainly not as straightforward as it might have seemed at first sight. The answer has to rest on a careful and (as far as possible) dispassionate description of all that has evoked the words 'religion' and 'religious' in order to discern what family resemblances they have. That work of description is the first level of what is known, to use a technical word, as 'phenomenology', that is, describing the phenomena while putting on hold or 'bracketing out' (*epoche*) judgements of truth or value.

There is no space to do that here, though there are many other books (including several of my own, e.g. *Beliefs that Changed the World*) which try to make a contribution to that work. The work of description has to be assumed here as the background to the question: if the separate organizations of belief and behaviour that we call 'religions' have sufficient family resemblances to link them together in Wittgenstein's interlocking and interconnecting ways, why have they taken such different forms? And if there are such differences, are they significantly real or are they a matter of appearance only?

Let us begin to answer those questions by joining a nineteenth-century traveller, Joseph Wolff. He was a great traveller at a time when that could be formidably difficult.

So why did he set out on his journeys? On one occasion he went to central Asia in order to rescue two hostages. More often he went because he wanted to argue. As Fitzroy Maclean put it in his engaging book, *A Person from England* (pp. 21f.):

> Wherever he went, Wolff argued. He argued with Christians and Jews, with Hindus and Mohammedans, with Catholics and Protestants, with Sunnis and Shias. He argued about almost everything: about the Pope, and the Millennium, and Mohammed, and the Lost Tribes, and the Second Coming, and the end of the World, and about what would happen to all fishes when the sea dried up.

On his way through Arabia he engaged in a series of theological discussions, which, even by his standards, were unusually lively. One was with some Wahhabis to whom he had given some copies of the New Testament. According to Palmer, in his life of Wolff (p. 198),

> he soon found that they were in a hostile temper which boded nothing good. 'The books you gave us,' they declared, 'do not contain the name of Mahomet, the prophet of God!' 'This circumstance,' he said, 'should bring you to some decision.' Their reply was curt and decisive. Wolff was sharply told that they *had* come to a decision, and any gloomy anticipations he may have had were abundantly realised. They seized him, horsewhipped him tremendously, and then went about their business.

Notice that he was arguing about issues that arise in and between religions, particularly the three 'religions of Abraham' (Judaism, Christianity and Islam), so-called because Abraham (Ibrahim in Islam) is regarded as the friend of God and the ancestor of all the faithful.

How, then, does it come about that so many religious people are prepared, not just to 'horsewhip each other tremendously', but to do far worse things than that? Wars, terrorism, persecution, slavery, domination of one class over others, control of women by men – all these (and much else) have been allowed and even commanded by those who have authority in religions. Sometimes that authority and those commands are deeply rooted in what is believed to be Revelation, so that they become in effect the word and command of God.

Of course religious believers have done many other things also. Some have certainly done things that are cruel and wrong – and religions are well aware of the nature of evil. But others have lived lives of generosity and integrity, of holiness and beauty. They have at times been pioneers of health and education; they have frequently led the fight against tyranny and injustice – often at the cost of their own lives. From religions has come an entire alphabet (literally from A to Z in the 13,000 entries in *The Oxford Dictionary of World Religions*) of things that we treasure and value, from art and architecture to Zen and zoology – since in origin what we now call the natural sciences came from the ways in which in the past religions sought to explain and understand the world.

Yet looking at the world today it is obvious that religions as social organizations (or more personally some religious believers) are involved in many of the most serious and intractable conflicts, as much in the present as in the past. Why has that happened? Why have there been such divisions and arguments among the many different religions in the world? Indeed, why have there been so many different religions?

The easy answer is to say that it is because there have always been so many people. They have lived at various times, in geographies and climates that often bear little resemblance to each other, and they have lived in separate communities. Those communities may be as small as a family or tribe, or as large as a city-state or nation or even an empire.

So through long periods of time, communities have lived in distinct ways which have been adapted to their own unique circumstances. Each community in its own environment has had its own history. It has developed its own memories, rules, customs and beliefs, and they are not identical to those of any others. The differences of environment, geography and resources have set a *limit* on the kinds of lives that people have been able to live. In other, more technical, words, the limits have constrained human lives into their various outcomes. Life as an Inuit on the edge of the Arctic Circle is very different from life as a Badu on the edge of the Sahara.

That observation gives us a first glimpse into why there are so many different religions, but there are, of course, many other constraints that set limits on what people can do if they are to survive and to flourish, and they too belong to any explanation of why there are different religions.

And here at once we are brought face to face with a major question, not just when we are trying to explain why there are different religions, but when we are trying to explain anything. It is the question, What counts as an explanation?

'Deep groans from the gallery', as Henry Irving once replied when asked how one of his productions in the Lyceum Theatre had been received. And deep groans here as well: do we really need even the briefest of brief digressions on 'explanation'? Why does it matter?

It matters because among the numerous accounts of what religions are, many offer bargain-basement explanations: they reduce the explanation to the lowest and simplest level even if that means setting aside what religions say about themselves. They are, in other words, reductionist. But is reductionism adequate as an explanation?

In everyday life it may seem to be so, because often in practice explanation does not have to be particularly complicated. When we are asked for explanations, our natural answer is to say, 'Because . . .' In other words, we try to identify the most obvious cause. Why did this book move? Because I pushed it.

But in fact there are many other conditions or constraints which contribute to the reasons why the book moved as it did: without the laws of motion it might have flown off into space; without your having a reason to stretch out your hand it might have remained where it was. 'The cause', as Shakespeare's Julius Caesar says, 'is in my will.'

We need, therefore, to remember that there are not usually single, simple explanations of complicated behaviours – and religious beliefs and practices are certainly that. In addition to any immediate and obvious causes, there are always other contingent, as well as background or domain, constraints which should (at least in theory) be a part of any complete explanation. And the word 'constraint' is extremely helpful here, because it reminds us that when we are trying to explain anything, we need to bear in mind, not only the immediate (proximate) causes, but also the passive and background conditions which have a causative part to play.

This distinction between proximate and ultimate causes has long been recognized. In sociology, for example, Alvin Gouldner (p. 31) applied one aspect of it in distinguishing between domain and background assumptions – and both of those are needed in understanding the ways in which religions construct and operate their world-pictures (to which we will come in due course). To take another highly relevant example, Wilson (p. 63) has drawn attention to the importance of this distinction in evolutionary theory (quoting Mayr, pp. 101ff.) while at the same time endorsing the recognition of multiple constraints:

> Ernst Mayr is credited with emphasizing the ultimate-proximate distinction, although it has always been implicit in evolutionary theory; Nobel laureate Niko Tinbergen independently called attention to four questions that must be addressed to fully understand any given trait, concerning its function, mechanism, development, and phylogeny; Tinbergen's fourfold distinction adds a temporal dimension to Mayr's twofold distinction. As an example of development as a separate question, the vertebrate eye can be studied as a mechanism of vision in its developed form, without necessarily considering how the eye developed during the lifetime of the organism. The study of development per se is required for fuller understanding. As an example of phylogeny as a separate question, consider the placenta of mammals and the pouch of marsupials. Both have the same function of gestating offspring, but they are very different from each other because mammals and marsupials evolved in isolation from each other on different continents. In general, evolution is a historical process that seldom takes the same path twice, *a fact as important for cultural as for genetic evolution* [italics mine].

Those distinctions illustrate the fact that there are always innumerably many different constraints which belong to any explanation of why things happen or appear as they do – many constraints which control each human life into its outcomes, into its thoughts and behaviours and beliefs.

But life being short, we cannot possibly list them all. So in practice we cut down the explanations as far as we can in order to identify the most obvious or fundamental cause: the book moved be*cause* I pushed it. We may of course add some further constraints (the book moved because you wanted to borrow it and because I therefore pushed it in your direction), but we cannot possibly list *all* the actual constraints.

This means that when we offer explanations of why things happen or why things appear as they do, we are always having to *choose* which among the many actual constraints are the most significant and relevant, having eliminated those which in contrast are clearly wrong or even absurd. So when we are trying to explain anything, it is wise to remember that what we specify as an explanation is a *choice*. All too often we go for the most obvious and immediate, and overlook the contribution of other significant and true constraints.

Taken into the natural sciences, the pursuit of the most simple and fundamental cause to the exclusion of other possible (but, from this point of view, superfluous) causes issues in what is known as 'reductionism' or 'causal closure'. That means in effect drawing a boundary and thus making what amounts to a closed circle of explanation.

Of course it is sensible to seek the simplest or the most direct explanations, and appeal is often made to Ockham's Razor in order to cut out any additional but unnecessary reasons. As Newton put it, 'Nature is pleased with simplicity, and affects not the pomp of superfluous causes.'

But that becomes a fatal error when other contributory causes are *not* superfluous, but are necessary if we are trying to understand the complexity of, for example, human behaviours. To use Ockham's Razor to cut out everything in order to arrive at simplicity, and then to use simplicity as a marker for truth, only makes sense, as Nancy Cartwright once observed (p. 827), 'if one believes that nature *is* simple, and will appear so through the filter of theory and language'. That is why I wrote in *Is God a Virus?* (p. 104):

> Where additional constraints must be specified in order to account for an eventuality, nothing is gained by insisting, in the name of Ockham, on only one. A better principle is this: be sufficiently, but not recklessly, generous in the specification of constraints; or at least otherwise be modest in what you claim to be 'the true and only explanation'.

The failure to recognize this was the error of the widespread and dogmatic reductionism of the twentieth century. It enabled Francis Crick, a molecular biologist and Nobel prize-winner, to put forward what he called 'the Astonishing Hypothesis' (p. 3):

> The Astonishing Hypothesis is that 'You', your joys and your sorrows, your memories and your ambitions, your sense of personal identity and free will, are in fact no more than the behaviour of a vast assembly of nerve cells and their associated molecules. As Lewis Carroll's Alice might have phrased it: 'You're nothing but a pack of neurons.'

But that hypothesis is clearly absurd. It makes what we may well call 'the astonishing error' of supposing that if you identify what is *necessary* in explaining or accounting for some phenomenon ('you' or 'me', for example), nothing more is needed. Your joys, your sorrows and all the rest of it do indeed require 'the behaviour of a vast assembly of nerve cells and their associated molecules': they are *necessary* since without them you would be dead. But they are not *sufficient* to explain the quality of your emotions or the formation of your intentions, let alone the individual occurrences of your biography. Brain imaging now goes down to the level of atoms (see, e.g., Letokhov, Chupp), and they are as necessary as the molecules, but they are not sufficient to account for the complexity of human life. It is a fundamental mistake of reductionism to suppose that the word 'necessary' is the same as the word 'sufficient'.

Thus it is clearly possible to scan and map the parts of the brain that are engaged and active in those beliefs and behaviours that we call 'religious'. Those activities in the brain are certainly *necessary* since without them there would be no behaviours, religious or otherwise. It follows that the neurosciences can monitor and identify which parts of the brain are engaged when beliefs are held and put into action. In that strictly limited sense, part of the explanation of religious beliefs and behaviours can be taken down to the molecular level. But it is not *sufficient* on its own to account for religious beliefs and behaviours, despite the widespread and prevailing assumption that it is.

That is why it is helpful to use the word 'constraint' rather than the word 'cause' when we are trying to explain anything: the word 'constraint' is useful because, as we have just seen, it includes both the immediate and obvious causes as well as the passive and background conditions. This is of paramount importance when we are trying to understand what religions are and why there are so many of them. It means that among the many constraints that control religious beliefs and behaviours into their outcomes there are some that occur within the religious domain itself.

To assume, as Crick and many others do, that claimed religious constraints are always absurd and wrong makes it impossible to understand what religions are. If we are trying to understand religious beliefs and behaviours we have to pay serious attention to what religions say about themselves, and also to the reasons they give for what they are and for what they offer to the enterprise and understanding of life.

The reasons may be expressed in pre-scientific language, symbols and actions. It is all the more important, therefore, to take time *to understand what has evoked them.* For example, some of the constraints that religions and religious believers claim to be controlling their lives into their outcomes are not open to direct or empirical observation. They detect agents at work in the world and in their lives. They may claim, for example, that among those constraints are *karma, kami, qadr,* spirits, witches, ghosts and the like. In theistic religions there is likely to be a belief that the one ultimate reality, to which words like God, Allah and Brahman refer, is the source and goal of all being, the unproduced Producer of all that is. In the words of one of the Upanishads from India (*Taittiriya Upanishad* 3.1.1): 'That from which all beings are born, That by which, when born, they live, and That to which, when departing, they enter, desire to know That: That is Brahman.'

How this kind of 'agency detection' arises and what part it plays in religious life has become in recent years a major part of the study of religions, particularly when it is linked to the fundamental importance of Bayesian probability and predictive processing. (If this is unfamiliar, a useful place to begin is with Clark's *Surfing Uncertainty*, with its Bibliography; we will return in Chapter 4 to the importance of predictive processing in understanding religions.) In the past, there has been a widespread assumption that false beliefs in supernatural agents give rise to, or at least reinforce, religious beliefs, but the recent work of Andersen suggests that the reverse may also be true. His argument is that *existing* religious commitments may produce an expectation that there are such agents at work, and that the (false) detection of those agents confirms 'the teaching and narratives upon which the values of a given culture are built'.

It is clearly the case that beliefs of that kind causatively constrain into particular outcomes the lives of those who hold them. They do not become true simply because they are believed. As the philosopher Quine observed long ago (p. 7), 'The intensity of belief cannot be counted on to reflect its supporting evidence.' All of us during the course of a lifetime believe many things that turn out to be mistaken. As Michael Frayn once put it: 'The tone of most of the things we do in life is probably going to turn out to have been painfully unsuitable in the light of what happens later.'

On the other hand, the word 'false' is correct only in the naive and obvious sense that the language through which the personification of agency has been made is, in terms of correspondence, mistaken. But whether those or other religious beliefs are pointing beyond the inadequacy of the language in which they are expressed to whatever is actually the case is a central and major issue of truth. It cannot be foreclosed by a pre-emptive use of the word 'false'.

It is certainly not an issue that can be decided on the grounds that since religious beliefs are often expressed in pre-scientific language they must be false. No matter how pre-scientific the language, we always have to ask the fundamental question: what is it in human experience that has evoked and given rise to claims and beliefs of that sort? Beyond the first level of phenomenology (dispassionate description as summarized earlier on p. 19), that question is taking us directly to the all-important *second* level: what is it that has brought into being the phenomena which are, at the first level, being described? In technical language, it is the issue of ontology and truth.

Leaving on one side, for the moment, that second level of phenomenology, it is sufficient here to bear in mind that religious explanations (or for that matter psychological or sociological or anthropological explanations) cannot be dismissed or ignored simply on grounds of reductionism. Reductionist accounts of religion *choose* to ignore additional constraints. But no matter how pictorial or pre-scientific the religious languages are, they may nevertheless be pointing to decisively causative constraints. When those constraints are taken into human lives (i.e. when they are internalized), they effectively and powerfully control those lives into their outcomes.

The way in which humans internalize constraints as the foundation of their lives lies at the heart of any understanding of religious beliefs and behaviours. Each religion is a distinct social context in which people grow up and live, and each religion offers them the resources through which, in the company and sometimes under the control of others, they form their own beliefs and behaviours. Each religion does this by offering its own constraints of belief and practice, and when these are internalized (taken in and stored), they lead to the particular characterization of individuals and society.

It is true that the word 'constraint' sounds at first very negative and restrictive: constraints stop people from doing things – as in the famous *Punch* cartoon (Williams, R. E., p. 142) where a younger sister is told, 'Go directly and see what baby is doing, and tell her she mustn't.'

But in fact it turns out that, although constraints are initially restrictive, for that very reason they often become extremely liberating. As we learned long ago from cybernetics, constraints are the necessary condition of greater freedom. That can be seen with dramatic clarity in the natural sciences, particularly in physics and biology, but it is frequently true also in everyday life. If people are stopped from doing things that might destroy them, they are set free to live with more understanding and common sense. Children constrained by the hand of a parent will not be run over by a car. Their lives are preserved to do other things.

So the acceptance and internalization of constraint creates opportunities that otherwise would not be available. Think, for example, of what is involved in learning to play a musical instrument. It will require accepting and internalizing many non-negotiable constraints. Initially some at least of those constraints will be restrictive: those who do internalize the constraints of, for example, notation and scales, and of practice, find that they are constrained initially in their use of time and energy. But they also find that they are set free eventually to play, and even perhaps to write, their own music. Haydn introduced brilliant innovations into his keyboard sonatas, and he did so, as he once said, only because 'I sinned against the rules of harmony'. But to do that, he had first to know the rules.

That is simply one example of a general and fundamental truth: the internalization of constraints prevents us from doing many things, but it leads to far greater freedoms. Constraint is the condition of freedom. The demands and the importance involved in the internalization of constraints are a reason why education, in a multitude of different forms, is so fundamental in religions. So also is the learning and practice (the internalization) of such things as prayer, yoga, meditation, zazen, worship and contemplation. As the Reform rabbi, Lionel Blue, once put it, 'Give as much time to God as you would to learning the guitar.'

From all this we can see why it is that those people and communities that live *perceptively* within the limits of constraint are able to survive and flourish. If they do so, they build up customs, beliefs, traditions and memories of how and why that has happened, and they certainly take trouble to pass on their accumulated wisdom to their children.

So it comes about that groups of people, living within the constraints of their particular circumstance, have formed their pictures and understandings of the world in which they live. To use a technical word, religions are, like the natural sciences, iconocosmic.

Clearly, the 'pictures' that religions and the sciences make of the cosmos are different in many ways, as much in method as in purpose. It does not follow, as many still seem to assume, that there is a major conflict between something called 'Science' and something called 'Religion'. That error ignores the reasons why Wittgenstein warned against generalizations of that kind, and it creates what Rudwick has called (p. 299) 'the "Anglophone heresy" of a singular "Science"'. In fact, there are many different and often positive ways in which the varying sciences and religions are related to each other (eight of them are summarized in *Why Religions Matter*, pp. 48–51). Certainly there *can* be a conflict if the claim (known as 'scientism') is made that sciences alone lead to valid truth, or if the claim is made that a text or teacher has such inerrant or infallible authority (for example, in revelation from God) that they cannot be challenged by any scientific claims.

A clear example of that can be seen in the way *some* Muslims deal with apparent conflicts between the Qur'an and some particular scientific claims. When I interviewed Muslims for a series on Islam for the BBC World Service (now in the book *What Muslims Believe*), I asked whether there can be conflicts between what the Qur'an says about human origins (i.e. Adam and Eve) and what is claimed in evolutionary theory. The consistent answer was that there cannot be conflict because the Qur'an cannot be in error. I asked one contributor, 'If it [a theory of evolution] conflicted with the Quran, would it, *ipso facto*, be false?' He answered (p. 157):

> Certainly those parts that conflict with the Quran would be false if they involve something basic and fundamental, and not just an interpretation (we must be clear that what we are saying is 'from the Quran') – but if there was something in the Quran which contradicted what Darwin has said, then we would not accept the theory, but we would accept the fact, and that is the Quran.

Not all Muslims would agree with that statement, but for those who do, it becomes a question of how the secular and the Qur'anic can belong together. A notable attempt to answer that question has been made in recent years by Fethullah Gülen. He founded the movement usually known as Hizmet, 'service' of others and of the world. (This is the movement condemned and attacked in Turkey by

President Erdogan as the cause of the attempted coup in 2017.) One of the main purposes of Gülen's movement is to show how Islam and the sciences belong together. As Caroline Tee has summarized the point (pp. 57f.):

He recognises that any *medrese* [*madrasa*] system of Islamic education, which focuses entirely on the study of Islamic texts and traditions, is unsuited to a modern age that is defined in large part by scientific progress. Equally, he is dissatisfied with a scientific education that is divorced from religious faith and thereby fails, in his view, to instil moral and ethical values in its students and in their scientific world-views. In response to this situation, his vision is a model of education 'that will fuse the religious and scientific knowledge together with morality and spirituality, to produce genuinely enlightened people with hearts illumined by religious sciences and spirituality, minds illuminated with positive sciences'.

So how does Gülen deal with the issue of an apparent conflict between evolutionary theory and the Qur'anic account of Adam and Eve? Very simply by rejecting evolutionary *theory* as unproven and therefore as bad science (see Tee, pp. 87–9).

But that kind of distinction between scientific theory and fact is grievously mistaken, as Martin Rudwick makes clear in his indispensable work on the long history of how successive generations achieved the recognition of evolution through the interaction of fact *and* theory (p. 298):

This distinction between the historical evidence for evolution (sometimes misleadingly called 'evolution as a *fact*') and its causal explanation ('evolution as a *theory*') is just one example of what has emerged repeatedly during the discovery of the Earth's deep history. Establishing the historical reality of *any* event in the deep past – not only those involving living organisms – has always been distinct from finding an adequate causal explanation for it. Again and again in the course of geological research, the reality of a past event, or series of events, has been established well before its cause or causes were fully understood; again and again, those arguing the events did happen have had to insist that the lack of a convincing cause for them was no reason to deny their historical reality.

There are, of course, other ways in which Muslims evaluate evolution, and Howard, in his extensive survey of 'the impact of the evolutionary worldview' on Islam, lists 'four modes of engagement' (pp. 157ff.). Among them are those who follow the many passages in the Qur'an which encourage people to look at the wonders and beauty of the created order and to discern there 'the signs of God'. For them, the sciences are one of those 'ways of looking'. On that basis, Howard goes further and suggests that Islam can make its own positive contribution to evolutionary theory (p. 171):

An Islamic contribution might push its anthropological vision to the fore. Side-stepping the occidental predilection for an individualist bias, it might make its own a basic intuition of post-evolutionary anthropology that there is no such thing as man on his own but only man-in-the-world and, one might add, man-in-society. Repeatedly, our study has shown that Muslims locate human uniqueness in those aptitudes – language, culture, etc. – which draw people together to one another and to God. According to Islam, where there is community there is also guidance; this is the point at which revelation history might enter the discussion.

That is simply a brief illustration of a far wider and more general truth, that many Muslims do not share the view exemplified by Gülen. But for those who believe that there cannot be conflict between the Qur'an and the sciences because any apparent conflict will always be resolved in favour of the Qur'an, secular education can seem extremely threatening. For them, the basis of education lies in learning and putting into practice the foundations of a Muslim life. That is why the First World Conference on Muslim Education, which was held in 1977, was entirely clear what the aim of Muslim education is: 'The ultimate aim of Muslim education lies in the realization of complete submission to Allah on the level of the individual, the community and humanity at large.'

That is clearly very different from the ways in which other religions define the purposes of education, and it led to the so-called Trojan Horse enquiry into certain state schools in Birmingham and elsewhere in the UK to investigate whether Salafi Muslims were attempting to 'introduce an intolerant and aggressive Islamic ethos'; the enquiry reached the conclusion (contested by some: see, e.g., 'Trojan Horse') that there was a 'sustained co-ordinated agenda to impose segregationist attitudes and practices of a hardline, politicised strain of Sunni Islam'.

For all religions, not just for Islam, there is a constant challenge to balance the issues of authoritative teaching with freedom of thought and research, and in each religion, including Islam, there are many different ways in which that has been done. (Those issues in the religions are effectively described in Gates in a survey which (p. ix) 'focuses on the nature and sources of authority in each of six major religions and on how freedom is perceived in each of them'.)

The consequent differences are irreconcilable, and they extend far beyond the immediate issues of the syllabus and of the school as community. To take another example, should Councils ban the supply to schools of unstunned meat, the kosher and halal meat that Jews and Muslims require, in response to the joint opinion of the RSPCA, the British Veterinary Association and the Humane Slaughter Association that 'the only humane way to kill an animal is to stun it'? When Lancashire County Council voted to do so, the acting chief executive of the Council, Abdul Qureshi, advocated that children should boycott their school lunches since the RSPCA's opinion 'is most of the time based on feelings, it's not scientifically conclusive' (*Daily Telegraph*, 27 October 2017, p. 11).

Within and between religions, therefore, there are widely differing ways in which sciences and secularism are evaluated, and it is certainly the case that they lead to extremely different consequences in social and individual life.

What at least the iconocosmic pictures of the sciences and religions have in common is that they are a consequence of the common human desire to explore and understand the world we live in. No matter how different the pictures created in the religions and the sciences may be, they are a consequence of a willingness and a determination to explore what the world is, and to find a way through the challenges and difficulties (known collectively as the compounds of limitation) which always and constantly face them. They share in common the capacity for imagination and wonder. When Richard Feynman was presented with the Nobel prize for physics, he said in his acceptance speech (Feynman, p. xxiii): 'Imagination reaches out repeatedly trying to achieve some higher level of understanding, until suddenly I find myself momentarily alone before one new corner of nature's pattern of beauty and true majesty revealed.'

A religious believer might well say the same. Where religions are concerned, the constraints in each case are so different that the pictures and understandings are different also. The widely varying constraints have meant that in each society the shared memories of the past, the lifeway and beliefs in the present, as well as the plans for the future have been varied and diverse. Each has formed its own strategies and has dreamed its own dreams of what the future may hold, and each has organized the ways in which as a society they must live together. In each community people are drawn together in shared structures, beliefs and practices which in turn then act as constraints in the forming of their lives. It is those coherently organized ways of living that we call 'religions'. But what makes them specifically 'religious' in contrast to other coherently organized ways of living such as the political, the social or the economic? In fact they all interconnect, as we will see shortly.

2

Do differences make a difference?
From genes to the Golden Rule

Already it begins to become clear why there are so many different religions: the massive variations of time and circumstance are bound to make a difference to the beliefs and practices around the world that we call 'religious'. But do they make *so much* difference that they must lead not just to arguments but all too often to actual conflict between and within religions?

One answer to that question is to say no. Certainly there are differences among humans in their histories and circumstances, and thus in their beliefs and practices. But, according to this answer, religions have much more important things in common than they have in dispute. As Shylock famously observed in *The Merchant of Venice* (iii.1):

> I am a Jew. Hath not a Jew eyes? hath not a Jew hands, organs, dimensions, senses, affections, passions? fed with the same food, hurt with the same weapons, subject to the same diseases, healed by the same means, warmed and cooled by the same winter and summer, as a Christian is? If you prick us, do we not bleed? If you tickle us, do we not laugh? If you poison us, do we not die? And if you wrong us, shall we not revenge?

If that is so, if humans have so much in common, how does it come about that some insist on making their own beliefs and practices a basis, even a reason, for attacking the beliefs and practices of others? Why are Buddhists among those attacking Rohingya Muslims? Why were Da'ish Muslims attacking Yezidis? How did it come about, to take an obvious example, that for so many centuries so many Christians conducted what Dagobert Runes called *The War against the Jew* (p. 82)?

> No group or nation or alliance of nations in all known history has ever perpetrated on a hapless minority such sadistic atrocities over so long a time as the Christians have on the Jews. Not one denomination or another, but *all* did, and especially those of the Catholic faith.

All religions, including those with the strongest commitment to peace, to non-violence and to the love of one's neighbour, have been involved in wars and conflicts. It would be totally wrong to say that religions are the sole cause of them, but it would be equally wrong to claim, as many do, that it is not religions but the perversion and corruption of religions that are the cause. In all religions there are specifically religious reasons, narratives and commands that require and justify in some circumstances engagement in conflict.

To take a current example, the Muslims involved in terrorist and other violent acts (such as beheading captives) have been denounced, not least by other Muslims, as 'not true Muslims'. It is argued that the ways in which they have been conducting Jihad (the struggle, both moral and actual, on behalf of God) are far outside the rules for Jihad established in Qur'an and Sharia.

But these so-called 'perverters of Islam' believe that they alone are putting into effect the true and earliest meaning

of Islam. In their view, they are following the example of
the Muslims of the first three generations of Islam, al-Salaf
al-Salihin (the wholly observant ancestors), from whom
the name Salafi is derived.

There are many different forms of Salafi Islam but,
among them, are some who see it as their responsibility
and obligation to be militant in their attempt to establish once more 'the true and earliest meaning of Islam'. In
recent years, they have been called 'Salafi-Jihadis' in order
to distinguish them from Salafis in general.

Salafi-Jihadis and other Muslims agree on very much,
but between them there is a deep and serious division
which affects the way Islam is lived and the ways in which
Muslims and non-Muslims can live together in the world.
It is a difference within Islam which goes back to the
earliest days immediately after the death of the Prophet
Muhammad (632 CE). Salafi-Jihadi Muslims believe that
they alone are the true Muslims, and that they have an
obligation to kill not only non-believers who have attacked
Islam but also apostate Muslims – in effect Muslims who
disagree with them. Believers who will enter the Garden
(of Paradise) are defined in Qur'an 9.111 as 'those who
fight in the cause of God, and who kill and are killed'.
What for others (including many Muslims) is an act of
terror is for them an act of faith.

At the heart of this division among Muslims is the fundamental *religious* principle in Islam known as *alwala'*
wa'lbara', roughly meaning loyal friendship and hostile
enmity (Shavit translates it as 'loyalty and disavowal'). That
principle (as Maher points out in his illuminating book,
Salafi-Jihadism) is used as 'a tool of "in-group" control which
draws a line against those deemed to be outsiders' (p. 111):

'It forms a distinct delineation between the Salafi-Jihadi constructions of Islam and everything else, forming a protective carapace around the faith which guards against impurity and inauthenticity' (p. 111).

That is an example of a division and conflict with specifically religious roots which has been going on intermittently since the beginnings of Islam. The conflict has been brought about and sustained by a compound of constraints (economic, political, social, psychological, geographical and so on), but among them are specifically religious constraints. The particular beliefs and practices of some Muslims are among the constraints that lead them to attack others – not only non-Muslims but other Muslims as well.

We can see from that example that although humans do indeed have much in common, they may also be divided from each other for reasons that are deeply embedded in their religions. Those religious reasons act as a constraint in the forming of actions and attitudes even for those who do little or nothing about the religion in question. Religions have been so important in human life and history that they have been the context in which most people have lived their lives – as indeed they still do, no matter how much or how little they are themselves involved.

So if we want to understand why there are so many different religions and why those differences can lead to contest and conflict, we have first to answer the question: why have religions been so important in human life and history?

To answer that, we have to understand how deeply religions are embedded in human evolution. That may seem at first sight a surprising place to start, because when we talk about religions, we usually think of such things as beliefs (God, Buddhata, Karma), structures (temples, synagogues, churches), people (gurus, saints, prophets), texts (Guru Granth Sahib, Qur'an, Bible), festivals (Christmas, Divali, Passover) and organizations (sects, sangha, cults). Those and so many other similar features enable us to pick out and identify those 'family resemblances' that we call 'the religious'.

But if we are to understand why religions are virtually universal (why, that is, they appear in every human society), and why they appear in such different and sometimes hostile forms, we have to begin much further back.

We have to begin with the basic observation that all animals, including humans, have to be *problem-solvers* if they are to survive. The problems that have to be solved are legion. Some are specific, immediate and particular, such as, for example, getting food for the next meal, finding a mate or dealing with a threatening enemy. Others are general and constant, including the effect of what we might describe *very loosely* as 'the laws of nature' like gravity, the conservation of energy and the equations of accelerated motion.

Anyone trying to find a way through a particular problem is not likely to think about (or perhaps even know about) the contribution made by the relevant laws of nature, but these nevertheless set a limit on possible solutions: they act as *constraints*. In general, therefore, the challenges facing problem-solving animals (including humans) can be summarized as 'the compound of limitations'. In any circumstance some limits are immediate and contingent, but they are set in the context of the general and background conditions of existence.

This means in effect that problem-solving animals have to find, if they can, a way through the compounds of limitation and constraint in which they live. If natural selection leads through competition to survival of the fittest, it is not surprising that all animals including humans organize themselves to enhance their chances of surviving; and in this context, 'survival' in its most basic and limited sense means surviving long enough to replicate genetic information into another generation.

Since 'the survival of the fittest' through natural selection has become a metaphor to justify aggressive behaviours in politics, business and economics (amongst much else), it is important to remember that Darwin himself disliked the phrase 'natural selection'. In 1860, in a letter to his friend Charles Lyell, Darwin wrote that he preferred the phrase 'natural preservation'. To preserve a social group is far more important for the survival of genetic information than a selfish battle against all competitors.

Religions are early cultural systems in which the protection of birth and the upbringing of children have been secured. Throughout human history – and often, still, in the present – religions have been the social context in which gene replication and the nurture of children have been protected. But there have been many different ways in which that has been done.

Our ancestors, obviously, did not have our knowledge of genetics, but that is beside the point in terms of evolution and natural selection/preservation. In those terms what matters is the protection and transmission of genetic information into another generation. It is only by passing on genes, and looking after children well enough to bring them to maturity, that human communities can continue through time.

That is why Darwin's preference for the word 'preservation' is so important. Religions are the organized contexts in which (amongst much else) gene-replication and the nurture of children are preserved.

In itself, this is an important reason why many religions are so concerned with sex and food. The rules developed in a cult/culture tell people what to do and what not to do. They tell them, for example, which foods are prohibited and which are allowed, which kinds of sexual behaviour are prohibited and which are allowed. In particular, they often control the status and activities of women very carefully so that the genealogy (also important in religions) of each child is clearly known.

All this made sense when so little was known about reproduction and when life was hazardous, especially for infants and children. The fact that much of this has come into question now that contraception enables couples to have sex without conceiving a child, or that DNA identifies parents much more accurately, does not affect the fact that for thousands of years religions have been the best systems that human beings could devise to ensure survival and community. And we are proof that they did it well! Here we are, the survivors of the survivors.

So far, this is the account of evolution that led Richard Dawkins to put forward the theory of 'the selfish gene'. But that theory and that metaphor of 'the selfish gene' are disastrously wrong. They make the elementary error of confusing the unit of retention (the gene, the unit that retains the DNA) with the unit of selection (the bodies that must survive long enough if any genes are to be transmitted). It is bodies that must be preserved if genetic information is to be transmitted.

For that reason, animals including humans organize themselves in communities larger than the family (in shoals, flocks and herds, for example) in order to preserve a group rather than individuals on their own. Often that involves, on the part of individuals, not selfish but self-sacrificing and altruistic behaviours which frequently contradict the idea of 'the selfish gene'.

There is, of course, an obvious sense in which it is true to say that the gene is a unit of selection, but not with the attributes of purpose and attitude that the word 'selfish' implies. Genes are not, as Oyama put it in her landmark work, *The Ontogeny of Information* (p. 40), 'diminutive chemical engines powering biological processes'. They are, rather, parts of a process. It would, therefore, be wiser by far to abandon the false metaphor of 'the selfish gene' and speak instead of 'the *selfless* gene'. The 'selfless gene' is far more accurate because genes do not have a self with which to plan and decide whether to act in a selfish or unselfish way. As Calow summarized the point (p. 120): 'The message passing along the communication channels established by the self-replicating systems (from one template to another) was, and still is, basically very dull and very simple – being just "transmit me".'

In fact, to quote Deeley, 'even that is a metaphor: a gene codes for a protein, which may or may not affect the likelihood of survival of the organism depending on many other conditions and constraints'. Thus the process involved is far more complicated, as Oyama makes clear (p. 39):

> What we are moving toward is a conception of a developmental system, not as the reading off of a pre-existing code, but as a complex of interacting influences, some inside the organism's skin, some external to it, and including its ecological niche in all its spatial and temporal aspects,

46

many of which are typically passed on in reproduction either because they are in some way tied to the organism's (or its conspecifics') activities or characteristics or because they are stable features of the general environment. It is in this ontogenetic crucible that form appears and is transformed, not because it is immanent in some interactants and nourished by others, or because some interactants select from a range of forms present in others, but because any form is created by the precise activity of the system.

Oyama's work is yet another example of why it is so important to think, not of single causes or agents, but of multiple constraints. What remains true is that 'the selfless gene' plays its interactive part in the building of bodies that do have a self, and which, therefore, *can* engage in unselfish as well as selfish behaviours.

Once we recognize how confused and wrong the metaphor of 'the selfish gene' is, and when we use instead the far more accurate metaphor of 'the selfless gene', we can begin to see why there are religions and why there are so many of them. Religions emerged in early human history as organized communities in which individuals (the units of selection) are connected to each other in mutual (though not necessarily voluntary) support. As a result society and individuals are protected and preserved.

There is a vast and varying number of ways in which that protection and preservation can be achieved – and that, yet again, helps to explain why, among the religions, differences are combined with family resemblances. Among those 'family resemblances' are the endorsement and encouragement of altruism. Indeed, one of the great achievements of religions has been to extend the boundaries of altruism.

Altruism can be defined as concern and action for the good of others (Latin, *alter*, 'other') even if it is costly to oneself. However, the nature and extent of altruism have become something of a battleground, not least because those committed to the false metaphor of 'the selfish gene' have had to argue that altruistic acts, despite the fact that they *appear* to be for the benefit of others, are basically not so: they are simply one of many strategies whereby the chances of the replication of 'the selfish gene' are enhanced (for example, by people expecting reciprocal rewards, or by protecting others whose genes are related to their own).

That argument used to seem plausible because it started from the familiar fact that, at its most elementary, gene selection is made at the level of individuals. That is the first level of selection: either individuals survive long enough to replicate their genetic information or they do not. But that level of selection cannot explain why some individuals will give up their lives in order to protect others.

That leads to the second level of selection, known as kinship selection. The unit of selection is a set of genetically related individuals, who thus create a kind of 'extended family'. In a set or group of this kind (of genetically related individuals), the genetic information will be replicated even if some of these individuals sacrifice their lives to protect others. That behaviour became known as 'kinship altruism', and it led to the famous remark of the biologist Haldane, who wrote, 'I'd lay down my life for two brothers or eight cousins.'

It is now becoming clear that there is a *further* third, level of group selection known as interpopulation or interdemic selection. This is the level at which populations are diminished or even extinguished at different rates. At that level, there is great advantage to populations that contain individuals who carry genes predisposing them to support others even at their own cost.

'Altruism' is thus taken far beyond 'game theory' and the recent arguments about whether altruistic behaviours give a strategic advantage to any society that endorses or enforces them. Considerations of strategy are clearly important, but current research is far more profound than that: it is seeking to identify genes or gene sequences that contribute to behaviours on the part of individuals who carry them which enhance the probability of survival of the group as a whole. On that basis, *gene-connected* altruism goes far beyond the kinship family, and already that kind of extended altruism has been observed in animals.

One of the truly great achievements of religion has been to extend 'the extended family' even further. Kinship selection can speak comfortably of the extended family, and that accounts for kinship altruism. But what religions created were even larger extended families that went far beyond even the kinship group of actual relatives. The gene-connected altruism (summarized above) helped to make this possible, but religions then supplied the metaphors and the rituals, the ideas and the imperatives, through which even genetic strangers have been bonded together as members of a single (though metaphorical) family.

This extension of altruism means that people have been prepared to live and even if necessary die in self-sacrificing support of each other. In the end some religions have dreamed that the whole human race might be a single family – an Umma, as Muslims would call it, or the Body of Christ, as Christians would speak of it, in which, according to Paul, we are all members of one another (Ephesians 4.25).

49

Given the importance of altruism in religions, it is not surprising that the practice and theory of sacrifice have played such a large part in the history of religions, but it has meant many different things in different religions. It is true that it is defined in *The Oxford Dictionary of World Religions* as

> the offering of something, animate or inanimate, in a ritual procedure which establishes, or mobilises, a relationship of mutuality between the one who sacrifices (whether individual or group) and the recipient – who may be human but more often is of another order, e.g. God or spirit.

But, as I pointed out in *Beliefs that Changed the World*, a brief definition of that kind is pointing to an immense variety of beliefs and practices entered into for many different reasons and purposes. When the sign in a shop window advertising a sale proclaimed, 'These trousers are being offered at a great sacrifice', it clearly was not offering them to the local deities. 'Sacrifice' is found in virtually all religions and extensively outside them, but its meanings are extremely varied. It has been understood as a way

- of cleansing fault or sin;
- of dealing with misfortunes such as the illness of oneself or of another;
- of turning away the anger of a deity or of an enemy;
- of saying thank you;
- of offering to a deity or to another person a substitute for something that you owe them and is rightly theirs (for example, the life of an animal instead of the life of the firstborn child);
- of establishing through a meal with recognized rituals a union with God or with others in a community;

- of giving something in order to receive something in return, often summarized as *do ut des*, 'I give in order that you may give';
- of maintaining and participating in the whole cosmic order;
- of celebration;
- of dealing with violence and anger through catharsis (defined, in part, by Aristotle in *Poetics* as leading through religious frenzy to healing and purgation);
- of accepting death in order to give life to others ('for your tomorrow we gave our today').

It is clear, therefore, that in the case of the word 'sacrifice', we are back in the domain of family resemblances. What at least it *is* possible to say in general is that the beliefs and practices involved in sacrifice have given dramatic expression to the ways in which people have to interact with others and with the world around them. In other words, people have to live constantly in the way of exchange that lies at the heart of sacrifice.

Of equal importance is the way in which sacrifice helps us to recognize and affirm that death is the necessary condition of life. That perception lies at the heart, not just of religions, but also of the scientific understanding of the universe: from the death of stars to the succession of generations, death is not simply 'end' but also opportunity. As I put it in *The Meanings of Death*, 'It is not possible to have life on any other terms than those of death; but where you *do* have death, there immediately you have the possibility of life.'

It is true that humans, including religious believers, are capable of great cruelty and evil, not least in the practice of sacrifice. But altruism reminds us that they are capable also of an immense and fundamental goodness that finds expression in a multitude of generous and loving acts. Recent research (see Crockett) has even identified parts of the brain that respond positively when a person chooses to act morally to help others (as opposed to harming them), thus contributing at least a small part of the answer to the question: why do people so often choose to do the right thing? Altruism is deeply embedded. On that basis, it is not surprising that the Golden Rule appears so widely. Confucius said (*Analects* 15.23), 'What you do not want done to you, do not do to others.' Jesus (among many others) put it positively: 'Do to others what you would have them do to you' (Matthew 7.12 NIV).

3

What does it mean to be human?

Altruism is a response to Shylock's plea that we should recognize how much as human beings we have in common, and how much therefore we should care for each other, even for the stranger in our midst. At an elementary level, Shylock was clearly correct. We do (generally speaking) have eyes, hands and organs, we do bleed if we are cut, and so on. Those common features are certainly taken up in religious beliefs. It is an important reason why there are the family resemblances among religions which give varying accounts of much that occurs to us all – the seasons, for example, the rising and setting of the sun, the distinction between sweet and sour, birth and death, past, present and future.

For that reason, it has been argued that there is only one ultimate and universal truth at the heart, or as the goal, of all religions. The many religions which appear in such a multitude of varying forms might then be regarded as different roads leading to the same ultimate destination or goal. As Radhakrishnan put it succinctly: 'The truth, which is the kernel of every religion, is one and the same; doctrines, however, differ considerably since they are the applications of the truth to the human situation.'

On that basis, there are many individuals and organizations seeking to develop a constructive and cooperative relationship between religions. Differences are not denied, but interfaith or interreligious dialogue is converted from words into common action. A good example is the way in which the 1993 Parliament of the World's Religions made what it called 'an initial effort – a point of beginning for the world sorely in need of ethical consensus' (*Towards a Global Ethic: An Initial Declaration*, Beversluis, p. 131):

> We affirm that a common set of core values is found in the teachings of the religions, and that these form the basis of a global ethic.
>
> We affirm that this truth is already known, but yet to be lived in heart and action.
>
> We affirm that there is an irrevocable, unconditional norm for all areas of life, for families and communities, for races, nations, and religions. There already exist ancient guidelines for human behaviour which are found in the teachings of the religions of the world and which are the condition for a sustainable world order.

The Declaration recognizes the many differences between religions (p. 133):

> We know that our various religious and ethical traditions often offer very different bases for what is helpful and what is unhelpful for men and women, what is right and what is wrong, what is good and what is evil. We do not wish to gloss over or ignore the serious differences among the individual religions.

But those differences, the Declaration argues, cannot contradict or destroy 'those things which we already hold in common and which we jointly affirm, each on the basis of our own religious or ethical grounds'. That is so because all humans share the same fundamental nature 'regardless of their social origin, sex, skin colour, language, or religion', and that is the basis on which the Declaration can affirm that there are 'binding values, convictions, and norms which are valid for all humans'. The Declaration therefore states, 'We are convinced of the fundamental unity of the human family on Earth.'

If that is so, then the many divergent accounts which religions give of who and what we are as humans are simply varying accounts of a common 'human nature'. On this view, the many different ways of being religiously human are variations on that common theme. They are diverse expressions of 'common core values', but the differences do not signal or demand a radical or disjunctive divide between them. In that case Jefferson and the Declaration of Independence are surely right to claim that certain truths (the six 'truths' in the Declaration of Independence) are so self-evident that they do not require argument or justification: they arise from and belong to a common human nature that is universal in its understanding of life, liberty and the pursuit of happiness.

But is it the case that there is a universal human nature beyond the elementary observations of Shylock? The view that there is a natural and good way of being human is often summarized as 'naturalism', although that word has several different meanings and applications. In general, however, naturalism rests on a belief that we can establish what we call 'human nature' on the basis of the ways in which we observe what humans characteristically do and think. Aristotelean naturalism, for example, believed that the best natural way for human beings to live can be decided from observable characteristics in much the same way that the best life for cats or for dogs can be discerned from observable characteristics.

If that is so, then it (human nature) would have a decisively important explanatory role in a wide variety of fields, particularly in ethics, politics and aesthetics – and also in religious beliefs and behaviours, because it could be used to support the claim that there are indeed 'common core values'.

But can we actually identify and define what is naturally common and good for all humans at all times and in all civilizations? Remember Wittgenstein's warnings about generalizations: 'This craving for generality is the resultant of a number of tendencies connected with particular philosophical confusions' (*The Blue Book* in Rhees, p. 17).

The point is crucial. 'Naturalism' could be helpful and useful only if there actually *is* a common human nature that is established on empirically observable characteristics; those in turn would have to be shown to be invariant across different cultures and forms of social organization, and invariant also through all historical periods in all parts of the world. For strong claims about that kind of naturalism to work, it has to do much more than tell us that people without food or water will die, or that they require sleep and oxygen in order to survive. It would have to include, for example, the consequences of brain behaviour in our thoughts, motives and emotions, the consequences also of the societies in which people live – in other words, in our mental, social, moral, aesthetic and spiritual life.

Otherwise, it is far too basic and rudimentary to support an argument that religions are nothing more than variations on the theme of a universal and common 'human nature'. The appeal to 'norms', as in the *Global Ethic* above, is not helpful, because norms are fundamentally statistical. To be ab-normal is simply to stand 'away from' (Latin *ab*) some statistical observation, although the word is now very often given a pejorative sense. The fact remains that an Aghori in a cemetery in Varanasi, a cardinal in the Vatican and a hunter-gatherer in the bush share basic and rudimentary features by being alive, but what it means to flourish, or to live 'the good life', or to be human, is for each of them radically different. Certainly they share many basic features in common, but their whole outlook, their motives, beliefs, concepts, hopes, evaluations, and above all their thoughts and behaviours, make them characteristically different as people.

This means that the accounts given by religions of what it means to be human (their accounts, in other words, of human nature, known as 'religious anthropologies') can be extremely divergent and can lead to dramatically different consequences for individuals and for societies. To take an elementary example: in some religions it is believed that there is such a radical fault in humans that they need to be rescued by a Saviour or Redeemer who does for them what they cannot do for themselves; in other religions, it is believed that while there is indeed fault and frailty, people can be educated or perhaps even coerced into goodness.

That and other similar distinctions may seem slight, but the consequences are immense in such things as politics, law, education and family life. Thus in India what is known loosely as 'the caste system' rests on the classification of *varna*, class, and *jati*, caste. Both of them are an expression of a *religious* anthropology, and they dominate and constrain life in every aspect. *Varna* is a part of what Brian Smith called 'the Vedic epistemological project of discovering the "connections" or "homologies" (*bandhus*) that can join components from different realms'. So he concluded

(p. 316): 'The universe can be classified into *varna*s because all of the components of the universe can be understood as bearing one or another of a limited number of what Wittgenstein called "family resemblances".'

Varna is deeply rooted in the Vedas (authoritative Indian Scripture), and although the exact relationship between *varna* and *jati* is disputed, there is no doubt that there is a close connection. So if we follow Smith's conclusion ('The *varna* system (in its social expression) comes to be a generalised, pan-Indic way of representing Hindu society; the *jati* is a more specific and localised method of doing the same thing', p. 318), we can see that Indian religious anthropology (including as it does continuing consequence in rebirth from one life to another) has had a decisively dominant consequence in Indian society. But the caste system was, and is, divisive – and the differences make a difference: quite apart from the often fierce disputes among Hindus, dissent from the underlying anthropology led (amongst other things) to the different religions of the Buddhists and the Jains.

Even from that brief example, we can see how consequential the different accounts of human nature can be, and how difficult it will be to arrive at a universally acceptable definition of what human nature or 'the good life' is: we find that what counts for 'good' in one culture or religion may be contradicted or even condemned in another.

Humans, generally speaking, do distinguish between right and wrong, beautiful and ugly, just as they distinguish between high and low, right and left. The ability to make such judgements is as basic and characteristic as other necessities that make life possible (homeostatic temperature control, digestion, an immune system and so on), but on the consequences and content of those judgements there is no common agreement. There is not even agreement on what counts as 'the good life' for cats or dogs: in some religions animals have souls, in others they are sacrificed; in some they are revered as divine, in others they are less than human and may be used to serve human purposes.

None of this variation is surprising since, as we saw earlier, religions arose in varying and changing contexts through long periods of time, and their beliefs, practices and organization were addressed, not only to the common and general limitations of life and death, but also to those that are specific, contingent and particular. The consequent religions have been winnowed and changed, but they carry with them much of the past from which they have come. Such common features as there are, the family resemblances, occur in such distinct contexts of constraint that they have produced the different organizations of belief and practice that we call 'religions'. The resulting differences occur not just between religions, but also within them.

So the problem of finding a common human essence and of defining a common or even universal religion based on family resemblances lies in the fact that what all humans have in common does not take us far enough into actual behaviours and beliefs. The same problem faced the United Nations when in 1947 it realized that its founding Charter needed to be more specific. It therefore drew up a Declaration of Human Rights which it called Universal. But from the start it was not universally accepted, and still it is argued by many that it is based on European perceptions that take no account of the ways in which different political systems or different religions understand what human nature is.

Thus Allott describes how, in horrified reaction to the Second World War, 'legal texts embodying "human rights" and "fundamental freedoms" sprouted like wild flowers in springtime . . . Overnight, as it were, *human rights* became an imagined entity with a prominent place in global consciousness.' But he then goes on to point out how 'all this well-meaning activity has given rise to a series of problems' – he lists 11, of which the ninth is that 'their [human rights] universality was always open to challenge on *cultural* grounds: they could be represented as derivations from a rather optimistic view of a particular cultural tradition'.

It could also be challenged from the point of view of particular religious traditions. That can be seen with startling clarity (to take only one example) in the 1990 Cairo Declaration on Human Rights, which makes it clear that 'All the rights and freedoms stipulated in this Declaration are subject to the Islamic Shari'ah' and that 'The Islamic Shari'ah is the only source of reference for the explanation or clarification of any of the articles of this Declaration' (Articles 24, 25). Sharia is 'the well-worn path' to be followed in life, and since it comes from Allah through the Qur'an, it cannot be altered. The Preamble states clearly the belief

that fundamental rights and freedoms according to Islam are an integral part of the Islamic religion and that no one shall have the right as a matter of principle to abolish them either in whole or in part or to violate or ignore them in as much as they are binding divine commands, which are contained in the Revealed Books of Allah and which were sent through the last of His Prophets to complete the preceding divine messages and that safeguarding those fundamental rights and freedoms is an act of worship whereas the neglect or violation thereof is an abominable sin, and that the safeguarding of those fundamental rights and freedom is an individual responsibility of every person and a collective responsibility of the entire Ummah.

This means in effect that the Muslim definition of rights, for example, regarding women and children (not least unborn children), may well seem to be in conflict with the UN Declaration. It is futile, therefore, for people to appeal to 'human rights' in the abstract as a non-controversial (because universally agreed) ground of protest because those protests do not consider which particular definition of human rights is being violated. That has been exemplified in recent years in protests against financial or trade dealings with Saudi Arabia whose human rights would necessarily be Sharia-based. As Evans and Evans make the point (p. v in their case studies of these issues around the world), 'There is an increasing gap between rhetoric and application. There appears to be little agreement on the meaning of human rights, especially on the issue of which rights have priority when claims are in conflict.' In his study of religions, rights and laws (with particular reference to the UK), Bradney gives particular examples of the problems involved in the case of marriage and family life, education, blasphemy, work and charity.

There are, therefore, many comparable conflicts in other religions which show how deeply differences make a difference in the accounts that religions give of human nature. They reflect a long-running debate in anthropology which actually led to some anthropologists opposing the drawing up of the UN Declaration on Human Rights. Anthropology is committed to field-work – to the long-term and close study of local societies (first level of phenomenology) in which contingent idiosyncrasies in culture and beliefs (in other words, differences) inevitably become apparent. It was important, therefore, that cultural relativism should not be destroyed by the imposition of so-called universal principles which come in fact from one particular perspective.

That point lies at the heart of the 'Statement on Human Rights' submitted by the American Anthropological Association to the UN Commission on Human Rights in 1947 (p. 539):

> Because of the great numbers of societies that are in intimate contact in the modern world, and because of the diversity of their ways of life, the primary task confronting those who would draw up a Declaration on the Rights of Man is thus, in essence, to resolve the following problem: How can the proposed Declaration be applicable to all human beings, and not a statement of rights conceived only in terms of the values prevalent in the countries of Western Europe and America?

It is true that the UN Declaration has been widely adopted, and it has been embodied in such legal systems as the European Court of Human Rights, based on the European Convention for the Protection of Human Rights and Fundamental Freedoms. It is true also that the recognition of 'human rights' is a massive achievement, a Copernican shift in human relations for which we owe much to the determination of Eleanor Roosevelt – of whom Adlai Stevenson once said in the United Nations (9 November 1962), 'She would rather light a candle than curse the darkness, and her glow has warmed the world.'

The Declaration remains, nevertheless, a human construction requiring consent and then enactment, neither of which can be taken for granted. Coming from a particular moment in human history it is not a timeless Absolute which must therefore be recognized and implemented by everyone. As Karen Engle commented (p. 559) on the 1947 Statement, 'The question is not now, nor was it ever, whether to be for or against human rights. Rather, the debate has always been over the definition of those rights.'

It is then a continuing work to translate ideals into particular laws and constitutions, and that can obviously be done in very different ways. Appeal can be made to the Declaration, much as Gladstone (p. 151) appealed to 'the law of nations' when denouncing the then Foreign Secretary, Palmerston, during the parliamentary debate on the Pacifico affair: 'I think it to be the very first of all his duties studiously to observe, and to exalt in honour among mankind, that great code of principles which is termed the law of nations.'

That 'law', however, is also a human construction (owing much, for example, to the work of Grotius in the seventeenth century), and it is, therefore, idle to appeal to it, or for that matter to human rights, as though they have an independent and unarguable existence. That is why William Blackstone, in his famous *Commentaries on the Laws of England* (4, p. 66), qualified his belief that the law of nations is universal by a recognition that consent is necessary: 'The law of nations is a system of rules . . . established by universal consent among the civilised inhabitants of the world.'

But that consent is far from universal. The recent work of Hathaway and Shapiro on the Kellogg-Briand Pact in 1928 (the Pact for the Renunciation of War) demonstrates how difficult it is to secure agreement on international law that will be universally recognized. Their book describes the long and contested work of human construction that led to (and beyond) the Pact, but it also emphasizes that it was never universally accepted (p. xi): 'You don't have to be an expert on international relations to know that the agreement signed that day – the Paris Peace Pact – failed to end war.' On the other hand, they argue that it did lead to a widespread recognition that *between states* war as 'politics by other means' has been replaced by sanctions – though the eight-year war between Iraq and Iran is a contradictory instance (p. xiii):

> The Peace Pact quite plainly did not create world peace. Yet it was among the most transformative events of human history, one that has, ultimately, made our world far more peaceful. It did not end war between states, but it marked the beginning of the end – and, with it, the replacement of one international order with another.

In a similar way, the UN Declaration on Human Rights is the result of a long process of human construction, and although it is widely recognized, it is not yet universally implemented. It is unwise, therefore, to appeal to 'human rights' as though they are embedded in a common human nature. That kind of appeal should never be used or imposed (as it often is) as though it is above and beyond argument. As Lord Denning observed (when hearing an appeal in the case of Waddington v Miah), 'It [the European Convention] is drawn in such vague terms it can be used for all sorts of unreasonable claims and provoke all sorts of litigation. As so often happens with high-sounding principles, they have to be brought down to earth.'

The problem of bringing human rights 'down to earth' lies in the fact, as we have just seen, that there is no universal agreement on what humans have naturally in common beyond the elementary. Certainly, there are enough 'family resemblances' to allow us to speak of 'humanity'. Even then, there are serious uncertainties about who or what belongs to humanity, as witness the debate about whether particular animals have rights, and if so, which – the question asked by Tom Regan when making *The Case for Animal Rights* (pp. 29–31). Michael Fox argued the opposite: he claimed that rights can only be attributed to humans, since they are (p. 52) 'reflectively self-valuing beings' and autonomous moral agents. But far from finding 'naturalism' a help to his argument, he found that its imprecision confused the issue:

Much has been written over the past few centuries on the subject of rights, and a good deal of this literature has mystified rather than clarified the concept. Probably the principal factor in this mystification lies in the traditional doctrine of natural rights. Natural rights are 'rights we are alleged to have in a state of nature, independently of human institutions and conventions, simply by virtue of our humanity (or some other set of attributes)' . . . Now the idea of a 'state of nature' is notoriously vague, and for all we know, one may never have existed, at least in the way envisioned by natural rights theorists, since *Homo sapiens* and their ancestral hominids have always been highly social creatures.

What we have in common at that basic level of humanity is undoubtedly fundamental and important. It includes the fact that the selfless genes, proteins, cells and so on build our brains and bodies in such a way that they prepare us for particular behaviours and, in a far wider sense, to be 'our selves'. The genes and proteins (to use that phrase as a shorthand) prepare us to eat food and to excrete waste, they prepare us to procreate the next generation, they prepare us to be aware through the senses of the world around us, they prepare us to feel emotions, 'the affections and passions' of which Shylock spoke, and to think about them. But they cannot create a common core of norms and values.

What is clear is that the genes may predispose individuals towards some particular behaviours, but they certainly do not dictate them. They contribute to the building of brains that experience emotions, some of which are so fundamental that they help us to survive: fear, for example, may trigger flight from danger – so much so that there is a direct pathway in the brain which connects that kind of emotion to rapid (almost instantaneous) response.

Even so, the emotion does not *determine* the outcome in any absolute or universal way: we might, for example, not flee but turn and fight; we might even *think* about the problem and, if we have time, try to talk about it together and work out the best solution. And there are in the human brain other pathways that connect emotional response to rational evaluation. In trying, therefore, to understand the interaction between emotions and motivation, it is clear, as Rolls and Treves showed long ago, that we are dealing with 'the operation and functions of a wide range of interconnected brain systems'; for a summary, see Rolls (1998) Appendix, 'Neural Networks and Emotion-related Learning'.

There is here a point of paramount importance in understanding what it means to be human in general, and what it means to be religiously human in particular. For centuries (or even longer: Lisa Feldman Barrett calls it 'the two thousand year assumption') it has seemed obvious that reason and emotion are separate systems in the brain, with emotion being prior to rationality in the history (we would now say evolution) of the brain and often in conflict with it. Feldman Barrett summarizes this (mistaken) 'classical view of emotion' (p. xi):

> Emotions are thus thought to be a kind of brute reflex, very often at odds with our rationality. The primitive part of your brain wants you to tell your boss he's an idiot, but your deliberative side knows that doing so would get you fired, so you restrain yourself. This kind of internal battle between emotion and reason is one of the great narratives of Western civilization. It helps define you as human. Without rationality, you are merely an emotional beast. This view of emotions has been around for millennia in various forms.

For the sake of balance it is important to remember that during those same millennia philosophers from the time of Aristotle onward have repeatedly questioned whether that account can be correct. They were constantly raising questions about the claim that 'reason is king over the Passions', as Cohen and Stern's brilliant philosophical history of their 'thinking about the emotions' makes clear. Those doubts powerfully support Feldman Barrett's conclusion (reinforced also from recent work in the neurosciences) that reason and emotion are so intricately connected and interactive that 'despite the distinguished intellectual pedigree of the classical view of emotion, and despite the immense influence in our culture and society, there is abundant scientific evidence that this view cannot possibly be true'. Her question about emotions then becomes inevitable (pp. 12f.):

> So what are they, really? When scientists set aside the classical view and just look at the data, a radically different

explanation for emotion comes to light. In short, we find that your emotions are not built-in but made from more basic parts. They are not universal but vary from culture to culture. They are not triggered; you create them. They emerge as a combination of the physical properties of your body, a flexible brain that wires itself to whatever environment it develops in, and your culture and upbringing, which provide that environment. Emotions are real, but not in the objective sense that molecules or neurons are real. They are real in the same sense that money is real – that is, hardly an illusion, but a product of human agreement.

From all this we can see that, while the genes and proteins build us so that we are prepared for eating and digesting, they do not dictate what we will have for breakfast tomorrow, still less how to earn a Michelin star; they prepare us for gene replication, but they do not dictate how we will behave sexually, let alone how to write and live the poetry of immortality and love.

That is why Thomas Hardy could use the word (p. 45) 'predestinate' of Jude springing across the room and out of the house in order to meet his 'enkindling Arabella'. The urgency of that constraint is familiar to us all, but it does not lead to only one outcome. We are prepared for gene replication, but the genes do not dictate only one consequence, since otherwise there would be nothing for a novelist to write about.

In those and other human behaviours, reason and emotion together are at work. It is true that whatever it means 'to be human' is necessarily gene-based, since otherwise we would not be alive, but (to repeat the point yet again) the genes *do not control* what any individual or group of people must do with this 'preparedness'. We are prepared for speaking languages, but the genes do not dictate what we will say in the next few minutes; still less do they dictate *The Merchant of Venice*. We are prepared for those beliefs and behaviours that we call religious, but the genes do not dictate what, if anything, we will do religiously.

So despite all that we have in common, to say that we are prepared from the genes for our various behaviours does not mean that the genes create one 'human nature' which all share in common. They may prepare us to be alive, but they do not tell us what that life is or how it should be lived; still less do they dictate what we do or think or feel.

The fundamental truth, therefore, is clear. The preparation from the genes and proteins is the *creation of opportunity*. It is not the dictation of consequence.

And that is why fundamental differences among humans (and eventually among religions) become inevitable and *are not in any way trivial*. The point here is obvious. In the human case the genes and proteins build brains of immense sophistication and competence in which reason and emotion work together. People are prepared from birth to learn and eventually to speak and communicate in languages in which feelings and emotions are at work together in both thought and communication. People are prepared and equipped to evaluate the circumstances in which they find themselves, they are prepared to imagine what the future may hold, they are prepared to experience the reality of love and even of God.

This means that in the human case, rational evaluation is combined with emotion in such profound ways that many different outcomes become possible; and that is true of all our 'affections and passions'. Shylock asks, 'If you wrong us, do we not revenge?' There are, however, many different answers that people give to that question. They do not agree, for example, on what counts as 'a wrong'. Even if they did agree some might say, 'No, we do not take revenge; we turn the other cheek.' As Sita told Hanuman in *Ramayana* (quoting, after the death of Ravana, the famous response of the bear to the tiger), 'You should not retaliate when another does you injury, even if those who do you wrong deserve to be killed.'

The truth is that not all human reactions and actions are as immediate and automatic as the blink of an eye. Many are the consequence of memory, evaluation and even, in some instances, of conscience – though even here there are differences between religions, as Chryssides concluded (pp. 195f.):

> My analysis of how Buddhist ethics works demonstrates why the concept of conscience rests uneasily with the Buddhist way of thinking. Yet it is important to note that it by no means follows that Buddhists are less concerned about ethics than Jews, Christians or secular humanists . . . It does not follow, either, that Buddhism has no place for remorse or repentance.

In other words, they may not have a specific equivalent to the concept and functions of conscience, but they could accept the observation (made long ago by Mark Twain) that humans are the only animals that blush – and need to.

This constant involvement of the whole brain/body is a reason why the commonplace distinction between 'the head and the heart' is so misleading. 'Headstrong' and 'heartfelt' are always at work together, even though either reason or emotion may happen to be dominant in any particular circumstance or moment – though 'dominant' is far too weak a word for those moments when emotions like rage and hate break loose from the leash of reason and 'let slip the dogs of war'; 'hot from hell' indeed. Nevertheless, reason and emotion cannot ever be entirely divorced from each other. In the same Act of *The Merchant of Venice*, the song asks:

> Tell me where is fancy bred,
> Or in the heart or in the head?
> How begot, how nourishéd?
> Reply, reply.

Religions are the reply to those questions. They map the ways in which reason and emotion are to be held together in the formation of distinctive character – so much so that together they create the sense of individuality, of the self being the subject of its own experiences and the agent of its own actions. The *personal* pronouns 'I' and 'you', as well as the plural pronouns 'us' and 'them', confer distinct identities which carry with them a value, often positive but equally sometimes negative and divisive.

This means that from the brains and bodies built by the genes and proteins emerge the individual properties of thought and feeling. They depend on the underlying chemistry and physics but they far transcend them. That is why religions speak of this characterized individuality in such terms as *atman, nephesh, jiva* or soul. Those terms are not synonyms, and they demand much careful analysis if we are to understand what religions mean by them. But what at least they do, at the first (descriptive) level of phenomenology, is confer identity and worth on each life. Indeed, in some instances they give undying significance to individuals.

Of course there are those, like Francis Crick (quoted earlier on p. 26), who take the view that words like 'mind' and 'soul' are empty because 'we' are identical to our brains and bodies: 'In short, the mind is the brain' (Dennett, p. 33). But, as Goetz and Taliaferro have pointed out in their lucid introduction to the arguments involved (pp. 190–4), that conclusion ('perhaps the most common objection to the traditional view of the soul', p. 190) is achieved by yet another illegitimate use of Ockham's Razor.

It is true, therefore, that our genetic inheritance acts as a constraint over what we are and what we do. Our genetic inheritance sets a limit on possibility. But, as we saw earlier, constraints, particularly when they are recognized and understood, become the condition of far greater freedom.

Thus, in the case of humans, the elaborate constraints that construct us set limits on what is possible, but they have set us free to understand and explore the worlds in which we live. We cannot live under water, nor can we fly to the moon (except in imagination) without rationally working out how to build a submarine or a rocket. We are then set free to explore the ocean depths and to fly to the moon. Our genetic inheritance does not in any way determine what we do or how we do it, but it does set limits which, when they are recognized and increasingly understood, allow the opportunity of *exploration* – the exploration of how to deal with the limitation, and perhaps even to pass beyond it.

Religions are the beliefs and practices that enable people in disparate groups to explore the worlds in which they live, and to face together the challenges and threats (the compounds of limitation) that face them, and then to explore what they are and what to do about them. In that way, religions have been the context in which the preservation of life and the exploration of the worlds in which people live have been most successful.

This means that religions have been the equivalent, in far wider and more general terms, of the submarines and the space capsules. They have been the vehicles in which people have been carried safely through time and perhaps even beyond time. They are the organized ways in which people have been able and encouraged to share their awareness and understanding (however limited that may have been at any particular moment) of all that stands in their way. Not surprisingly, each religion identifies particular constraints which it encourages or requires or even demands individuals to internalize.

It is on the basis of our internalized constraints that we learn to make judgements of good and evil. Yet again we can recognize that the genes and proteins (and much else) build us as the kind of animal that can make those judgements, but they certainly do not dictate what we as moral human beings will identify as good or evil; still less do they dictate what we will then do or not do.

It follows that much of what humans think and do depends on constant evaluation of what is right, or wrong, or helpful, or dangerous, or pleasing and so on, and those evaluations are not dictated: people in the same situation may come to completely opposite conclusions.

Even so, in the forming of those judgements, particularly in the case of moral and aesthetic judgements, there are conducive properties which evoke those judgements. (If conducive properties are unfamiliar there is a summary in *Why Religions Matter*, pp. 212–20.) That is one important reason why, *in general*, humans do recognize certain absolute values – values, that is to say, that remain what they are even though they occur in different, contingent circumstances. Work in the neurosciences in recent years has shown how and why judgements of good and evil, or of beauty and ugliness and so on, can be (albeit in a limited way) objective. They are not entirely subjective or relative, as some still maintain.

Not surprisingly, therefore, humans in general recognize truth, beauty and goodness. But the fact remains that they *do not necessarily agree* on what counts as true or beautiful or good. Indeed, they may passionately disagree and give strong and considered reasons why they do so – reason and emotion combined. Those disagreements occur, not just among individuals, but also among groups of people organized in some form of society and certainly, therefore, between and within religions. And the differences undoubtedly make a serious difference.

Each religion is thus a community of shared imagination and practice. It was the achievement of religions to create those shared understandings and cooperative behaviours in terms that met the demands of, internally, reason and emotion, and of, externally, social cohesion. The fact that there are different religions means simply that that can be done successfully in many different ways and with very diverse content and consequence in each case.

The key to that success was language. Language was the great achievement that made humans, in distinction from other animals, possible. In his breathtaking study of the history and spread of languages, Nicholas Ostler pioneers what he calls 'the study of *language dynamics*' or of diachronic sociolinguistics (p. 558). The jargon may be off-putting, but the work is of paramount importance:

> It is an approach, previously little explored, to understanding human societies: how language, in all its evolving variety, organises not just the human mind but also the large groups of human minds that constitute themselves into societies, which communicate and interact, as well as think and act.

It is language that enables the extension, and in the end the transcendence, of *elementary* cooperation. There are many self-replicating organisms that enhance their chances of survival by living together in cooperative communities, and they make much use of sound (sounds of alarm or of recognition, for example, in flocks of birds, troops of monkeys, pods of dolphins, and so on).

In a profound way, religions exploited the opportunities in sound, in varying musical notes, and eventually in language. It is a reason why Sound is so important in Indian religions. St John's Gospel starts, 'In the beginning was the Word'; we would start, 'In the beginning was Information'; Indian religions start, 'In the beginning was Sound.' If you study early languages, particularly biblical Hebrew, it is still possible to overhear the beginnings of language among our ancestors long ago as they turned sound into words – an observation powerfully reinforced by recent research showing that baboons, despite having the higher larynx that was previously thought to make the conversion of sound into language impossible, do produce five contrasting vowel sounds. They are 'a precursor to the vowel system universal in spoken human language', suggesting that 'languages evolved from ancient articulatory skills already present in our last common ancestor with Cercopithecoidea [one of the Old World monkeys], about 25 million years ago' (Boë *et al.*).

The achievement of language is most usually expressed in words, but it can be expressed non-verbally, in such things as signs, pictures, symbols, gestures. In religions, the creation of signs and symbols that people could recognize and share was decisively important. When these were combined with verbalized language, humans were able to extend vastly the nature and range of cooperation. They were able to express their ideas and emotions in increasingly ordered ways, leading eventually to the formation of shared beliefs.

That 'sharing' is ordered and formalized in the systems that we call (because of their family resemblances) religions. It was through language (non-verbal as well as verbal) that religions created the stories and the narratives, the rules, the rituals and the organization of families and societies, that have guided and controlled humans into behaviours (not least, as we have seen, in relation to sex and food) which have been rewarded in terms of survival, preservation and continuity.

What religions thus achieved is what is known as 'cognitive consensus'. People, in their own community and religion, are able to agree on what it is that they are looking at and give it a name, they can discuss what is happening, they can identify who belongs to which family, they can plan together how to get the next meal, and much else. And far beyond that, people can share together a sense of meaning and purpose in life, culminating in a final goal and destination – in Enlightenment, for example, or in a secure relatedness to God. It was religions that offered the ideas, narratives and rules, as well as the tools and techniques, of consensus in the shared and imagined worlds that they created.

Since each of those shared and imagined worlds has its own horizon of limitation and constraint, it is not surprising that the cognitive consensus in any one of those 'worlds' is different from that of others. Each religion creates and sustains its own distinctive and coherent picture of the world (of what it is, of where it came from, of how we should live within it), and each has its own core beliefs and practices giving it its own distinct identity and character.

It is not the case that the picture or the lifeway of any religion is static or unchanging; nor is it the case that all the people within it necessarily agree with each other or even with the picture itself, at least in all its details. That often proves divisive. The cross of Jesus, for example, is a fundamental part of the Christian picture, and yet there are many ways of understanding how the cross effects salvation. The different understandings of what Christians call atonement have led to contest and arguments, and even to conflict and separation among their churches.

As a consequence of all this, there are differences, not just between religions, but also within religions. This means that although people in any particular religion share much in common, there are many different ways of being a Hindu, or a Daoist, or a Christian, or a Jew, and so on. How is that difference to be handled? Huckfeldt called a society's capacity for tolerating political disagreement (the survival of diverse opinions within communication networks) 'a central issue in democratic politics'. So it is also (*mutatis mutandis*) between and within religions, and it can only be tackled by the immensely difficult creation of contexts in which people can disagree and still remain friends.

Equally to the point, religions are set in space and time where circumstances and understandings in the world at large are constantly changing. So religions repeatedly have to face the challenge of change. For some in any religion, major change is impossible: the truth and the tradition have been given in the past by inspired teaching, and perhaps ultimately by God in Revelation, so for them there can be interpretation, but it cannot extend to radical change, because that would make the word of God subordinate to human opinion. In contrast, for others the word of God enters into changing circumstances and transforms them, making changes that often challenge, not only human opinion, but also some parts of the received tradition.

Once again, we see why there are different religions and also differences within a religion. Even when there are variations and disagreements within a particular religion, most people still feel that they belong to the same general picture and will want to live out their lives as part of that picture, even though it may be according to their own interpretation of it. It is their way of seeing the world. They do not necessarily think about it in any great detail, but it still gives meaning, pattern and structure to their lives. Like the people of Santa Dulcina delle Rocce (in Evelyn Waugh's *Sword of Honour*, p. 5), 'the supernatural order in all its ramifications is ever present and ever more lively than the humdrum world'.

4

Exploring the worlds around us

All of us, from our earliest moments of learning and of internalizing constraints, build up our picture of what the world is and of how we should live and act within it. For many, that picture is religious. But whether or not that is so, our senses then receive unending streams of data which we either ignore or interpret according to the picture that we have internalized, and of course that picture is confirmed or corrected as we learn and grow up.

We do, therefore, make mistakes, but our internalized picture of the world in general, or of its details in particular circumstances, is *well informed*. The consequence of information is that all the near infinite possibilities in a universe of this kind are controlled into specific outcomes. Much of this is already stored and built into our picture of the world, and we thus become what Deutsch and Marletto (introducing the term 'constructor', meaning something, like a catalyst, that can cause a transformation while retaining the ability to cause it again) call 'knowledge creators':

> For almost any task that is possible under the laws of physics, the explanation of why it is possible is an account of how knowledge might be created and applied to build a constructor for that task. That makes knowledge creators, such as people, central to fundamental physics for the first time since Copernicus debunked the geocentric model of the solar system.

This takes us far beyond the brain being nothing more than a complicated computer connected to a robotic shell or body that executes its instructions. The brain does indeed compute, but it is also conscious and self-monitoring in such a way that, as Andy Clark puts it (p. xiv), it is able idiosyncratically to generate thoughts, plans, imaginations, dreams, 'a whole smorgasbord of mentality, emotion and intelligent action'.

Those words are taken from Clark's book, *Surfing Uncertainty*, in which he describes the key role in perception of predictive processing based on probability. What is known as 'predictive processing' is the ability of the human self (the subject of its own experience and the agent of its actions) to monitor and scan its environment in order, as far as possible, to predict what is happening. It is vital for our preservation and survival. It is also, as we will see, fundamental in understanding religions because for many people their religion is in effect their way of seeing the world and of acting within it.

Predictive processing means that when our senses are bombarded with data, we do not simply receive inputs or take in data like the lens of a camera. The analogy of the camera (misleading though it is, as we saw in the last chapter) is attractive for those who believe that the brain makes use of two separate and often competitive systems in our perceptions and responses. Thus Joshua Greene uses the analogy in order to argue for a dual-process brain (p. 133):

> The human brain is like a dual-mode camera with both *automatic settings* and a *manual mode*. A camera's automatic settings are optimised for typical photographic situations ('portrait,' 'action,' 'landscape'). The user hits a single

button and the camera automatically configures the ISO, aperture, exposure, etc – point and shoot. A dual-mode camera also has a manual mode that allows the user to adjust all of the camera's settings by hand. A camera with both automatic settings and a manual mode exemplifies an elegant solution to a ubiquitous design problem, namely the trade-off between *efficiency* and *flexibility*. The automatic settings are highly efficient, but not very flexible, and the reverse is true of the manual mode.

This leads Greene to write of 'emotion versus reason' (a chapter subheading, p. 134) and to describe reason as 'the champion of the emotional underdog, enabling what Hume called "calm passions" to win out over "violent passions"' (p. 137).

That analogy, however, is as misleading as the equally false metaphor of the selfish gene. Far from receiving data like a camera, predictive processing makes clear that we meet the data, so to speak, halfway. We bring our internalized picture of the world to bear in order to predict what is happening and to initiate appropriate response and action. In doing so, it is clear (as we saw in the last chapter on p. 67) that reason and emotion are not inevitably in conflict with each other, but are much more fundamentally integrated in the ways in which we live in the world and within ourselves.

This means that within our existing 'picture of the world' we already have beliefs and feelings supporting strategies that have served us well so far. It enabled Winston Churchill to tell Colville (p. 405) during the Blitz that 'he was not much worried by the chance of being bombed – in this connection he is fond of quoting M. Poincaré's statement, "I take refuge beneath the impenetrable arch of probability."'

But of course 'the arch' is *not* impenetrable. Because predictive processing is based on probability, it is obvious that we will make mistakes. When we do so, those mistakes can often be integrated into the existing picture and can if necessary change it. If the mistakes are more serious (if, for example, there is a repeated mismatch between prediction and perception), the consequences may be damaging. At an extreme, they may produce what Edwards, Adams *et al.* have called 'functional motor and sensory symptoms' (FMSS), including, to quote their examples, 'anaesthesia, blindness, deafness, pain, sensorimotor aspects of fatigue, weakness, aphonia, abnormal gait, tremor, dystonia and seizures'. They argue that what is known in computational circles as 'predictive coding' is rightly called 'generative' because it generates sensory predictions given probabilistic beliefs about their causes. Applied to the brain, the *failure* of predictions based on probability can lead to disabling symptoms which in the past might well have been called 'hysteria'.

Usually, however, the effects of predictive processing are less dramatic and more helpful. For example, when you are trying to talk to someone in a noisy room, much of what the other person says will be inaudible, and yet the brain fills in inaudible sections of speech because (as we now know from recent research: see Leonard) the region of the brain known as the left frontal cortex predicts what word you are likely to hear one-fifth of a second before the superior temporal gyrus processes the sounds you have heard.

Going back to the general picture, it is predictive processing that enables us to live successfully day by day. Take, as an example, going to work in the morning, an elementary 'compound of limitation' with which we are familiar. We stand at the bus-stop and scan the immediate horizon. We are already predicting the arrival of a bus, and we already have a picture of what it will look like. When the appropriate data invades us (i.e. the bus arrives) we know already how to act appropriately by getting on and finding a seat. From the picture reinforced from experience, we predict that there will be more room at the front than at the back and move appropriately.

In this example, we are prepared and ready to predict what should be happening from the picture we have built up from experience and learning, and from internal processing operations in the brain. Sometimes the predictions are wrong and we have to make adjustments. If a sinkhole opens up and the bus disappears from sight, we make immediate and different responses. We may, for example, run to see if we can help any people involved. But that reaction also belongs profoundly to the predictive picture that we carry within us.

This understanding of predictive processing changes dramatically our traditional understanding of perception. Instead of regarding the brain as a computer or camera passively receiving inputs, it sees the brain as an organizing and conscious agent (evoking such words as 'mind' and 'self') proactively scanning and monitoring its environment in order to anticipate what is happening and what we ought to do. Andy Clark, in his introduction to predictive processing, ends his book with this short paragraph (p. 300):

> The brain thus revealed is a restless, pro-active organ locked in dense, continuous exchange with body and world. Thus

equipped we encounter, through the play of self-predicted sensory stimulation, a world of meaning, structure, and opportunity: a world parsed for action, pregnant with future, and patterned by the past.

That is exactly what religions and the religious imagination have been supplying and sustaining supremely well throughout human history. They have built up powerful and coherent pictures of human nature, and of the world around. To pick up Clark's words in the paragraph just quoted, religions give

- *meaning* to time and experience, conferring on individuals significance and identity;
- *structure* to social organization from family to politics;
- *opportunities* and resources for people to live their lives 'on approval' – the approval immediately of those around them and ultimately of a final destiny, whether of Enlightenment or of God.

This means that religions are a consequence of the predictive processing that lies fundamentally within our human nature. We can see that clearly if we unpack in a little more detail the three phrases in the last words of that paragraph: a world (1) parsed for action; (2) pregnant with future; and (3) patterned by the past.

(1) Religions 'prepare us for action' by parsing and defining what the world is and how we should behave within it. The ethical consequences of religious belief are worked out, often in great detail, telling people what they should do in particular circumstances and in their social life. They define and encourage appropriate behaviour (called *dharma* in India, where Sanatana Dharma, 'everlasting dharma', is its

own name for its religion) and they strongly discourage the opposite with threats and punishments, including unending fire after death – or, in other religions, everlasting ice. The themes of judgement and accountability are a constant constraint in religious belief and practice, but what exactly that means in picture and practice varies greatly.

Not surprisingly, therefore, religions offer powerful resources to help or even to demand particular consequences in practice. Those resources (often mediated through authoritative guides like priests and gurus, or through texts, revelations and scriptures) range from goddesses and gods to rituals and sacraments. The nature and effects of those resources are described in languages and pictures that are often, if taken literally, remote from our own. Even so, it is important in understanding religions to try to discern what it is in human experience that has evoked the languages that personify causes in terms of ghosts, devils, angels, witches and the like. Personification of that kind helps people to interact with an otherwise opaque and mysterious world.

(2) Religions are 'pregnant with future'. Life is lived as project. People are conscious of the future but they know extremely little about it – hence the somewhat malicious definition of economists as people who tell you tomorrow why what they predicted yesterday didn't happen today. Religions have been active in attempting to penetrate that particular compound of limitation with such functionaries as prophets, soothsayers and seers, and with rituals and sacrifices.

Even more importantly, religions map and describe the world as they believe it should and will be – a messianic age in which 'they shall beat their swords into ploughshares, and their spears into pruning-hooks', to quote a Jewish example (Isaiah 2.4). The dream may be utopian (literally from the Greek, 'no place'), but religions encourage their people not just to dream but to take action, now and here, to make it real.

Being 'pregnant with future' is what is known as 'cultural prolepsis', the way in which religions lay out what the future will hold. They may, for example, describe the final and ultimate goal of time and process, and will then supply maps of how to get there.

As a result, religions are inclined to look not only to the present and the immediate future but also to a final destiny, which often takes the form of an apocalyptic future when the whole cosmos will come to an end – often a violently cataclysmic and destructive end in which the faithful will be safe but the unfaithful will perish. Not only that, but their predictions of this will be verified, with the result that the faithful may well be looking forward to being vindicated in this event. In the New Testament, the book known as The Apocalypse (Revelation is simply the equivalent Latin word) is a pregnant dream of that kind: 'Then I saw a new heaven and a new earth; for the first heaven and the first earth had passed away, and the sea was no more' (21.1 – the verse, incidentally, that gave rise to one of Joseph Wolff's arguments, as we saw earlier on p. 20, about what will happen to the fish).

(3) Religions, to go back to Clark's words, are 'patterned by the past' by drawing systematically on history and memories from the past and reiterating them in often-repeated myths, traditions, narratives and even scriptures.

When those texts and teachings are believed to be inspired and perhaps even revealed, the past enters the present in a way that reinforces the differences and divisions between and within religions. They act over beliefs and behaviours as a constraint which has authority. This can lead to such disjunctively different outcomes that the differences do indeed make a difference within religions, as we saw by way of example in the caste system in India and in the Salafi understanding of Islam. They make a difference also between religions, as we can see in India itself in the separation of India and Pakistan in 1947 – or, in another example, in the divisive evaluation of Jerusalem between Israelis and Palestinians.

Even beyond that, those texts and teachings from the past have to be interpreted, and the methods and consequences of interpretation (known technically as 'hermeneutics') are not agreed within religions, let alone between them. At one extreme there are those who insist on going back to the original text and relating it as exactly as possible to the present. In summary this can be called 'the hermeneutics of fundamentalism', but 'fundamentalism' is, yet again, a word with its own history and now with many, often contested, meanings. Hunter observed (p. 27) that 'scholars very often wince' and are aggravated 'by the cavalier, even sometimes reckless, usage of the term . . . as just another synonym for religious dogmatism or ideologically rooted authoritarianism of whatever historical manifestation'. In his view fundamentalism is one particular response of orthodoxy (defined as an achieved 'consensus through time') in confrontation with modernity (p. 28).

In contrast, there are others who accept that particular texts and teachers exercise the constraint of authority but they apply them as relevantly as possible to the changing circumstances of life (the hermeneutics of opportunity).

In a comparable way, the Constitution of the United States (which can be amended but not changed) is interpreted in different ways, leading to different judgements in the Supreme Court. The so-called Originalists go back to the text, either to apply what they take to be its original meaning, or to discern and apply the intention of those who wrote it; but others attempt to apply the spirit of the original to changing circumstances. There must be varying interpretations because, to quote Purcell in his book on Originalism and the American Constitution (p. 69), 'it was essential [for the Founders] to design a frame of government capable of adapting to the demands of an unknowable future'. The Constitution is open to different and even conflicting conclusions because it cannot determine which method of interpretation is correct.

It is a comparable problem of rival interpretations that leads to irreconcilable differences in religions. In any religion based on an authoritative text, there are text-Originalists who believe that there is an authoritative and original meaning that has to be implemented, and there are others who do not deny the authority of the text but who seek to apply the spirit and purpose of the original to changing circumstances. It is exactly as it is expressed in Liu and Schroeder – in the aptly named (in this context) *Keeping Faith with the Constitution* (p. 9): 'Beyond the original Constitution, subsequent amendments express commitments to *a series of fundamental values*, beginning with the Bill of Rights.'

In contrast to text-Originalists, the hermeneutics of opportunity do not betray 'fundamental values', but interpret and apply 'the spirit and purpose of the original' to the constantly changing world. This leads to irreconcilable differences within religions relying on authoritative texts on innumerable issues, ranging from the characterization of God and the universe to the status of women, children, education, animals, food and sex – not least in their consideration of gay relationships. And the many different ways in which authoritative texts can be interpreted clearly make a difference: 'The consequence has been not just disagreement but such contest and anger that it can lead to religious wars.' (See the summary of these deeply divisive issues in Additional text 3.)

Accepting the authority of a sacred text is only one of many ways in which religious participants live in the past. As a result, they often look back to a golden age, a *satya-yuga* ('age of truth') as Indian religions might call it, when there was perfect unity in belief and social order. We have already seen another example in the Salafi Muslims for whom the period of al-Rashidun (the first caliphs after the death of Muhammad) is 'the golden age of Islam'.

This means that religious memories are extremely long and are entangled in cultural and political memories as well, and they reinforce the reasons as to why there are different religions. We can see an example of that in the way the medieval historian Marc Bloch (an eminent historian of Europe who was himself executed as a Resistance fighter in 1944) wrote in 1940 of the Anglophobia of many Frenchmen after what they regarded as the British abandonment of France at Dunkirk (pp. 68f.):

Its causes are many and various. Some are linked with historical memories which are tougher than a good many people seem to think. The ghost of the 'Maid', the hateful figures of Pitt and Palmerston, have never altogether ceased to haunt a collective mind which is only too ready to remember the past . . . It must, I think, be regarded as inevitable that two nations, so different as ours are – different in spite of having in common many of their most fundamental ideas – should find it very difficult to know, to understand and, consequently, to love one another.

It is because the past is so important that sociologists and anthropologists have observed in religions what is known as 'cultural lag'. Religious believers are alive at some present moment, but they are always living to some extent in and from the past, because the great themes and metaphors that control and guide their lives are rooted in the past – such themes as atonement and forgiveness, salvation and enlightenment, pilgrimage and conversion, healing and hope. The psychoanalyst Carl Jung once observed of people who came to him for help that many of them were living in the year 5000 BCE, though a few rare souls had reached the Middle Ages.

So religions are 'patterned by the past' and 'pregnant with the future' in a world that is 'parsed for action'. On that basis, each religion creates its own shared (or at least 'shareable') understanding or picture of what 'the world' is. Religions are, as we saw earlier, iconocosmic. The pictures and understandings they create may well include utopian dreams, but they deal equally with the dystopian realities of life. They are concerned in particular with what we would call politics and economics – a reason why power and religion are so often connected in virtually all societies in the past, and often still in the present. The connection, however, is worked out very differently in each case. For example, what it produced in Europe during and after the Reformation is nothing like what it produced in Japan under the late Meiji emperors, particularly in the case of Hozumi Yatsuka (1860–1912), who established what Skya calls (p. 53) 'the religious, *völkisch* family-state'.

So the shared pictures in each religion produce widely differing and often competitive consequences. In general terms, however, the importance of shared pictures is that they have enabled humans to understand the compounds of limitation before them (including the ultimate limitation of death), and to predict and form strategies to deal with them.

Religions have thus been immensely successful as protective systems – so successful, indeed, that people living in those systems have been able not just to survive but to do many other things as well. Above all, they were – and still are – set free to explore their own nature as well as the world around them. The fact that our ancestors began to explore the world of their time, and to understand it better, explains, as we saw earlier, why the natural sciences are deeply rooted in religions. It is often forgotten that the natural sciences were originally a part of religious exploration. It is only in recent centuries that they have come apart as distinct, though obviously interconnected, belief-systems.

The exploration of the external world, particularly of the cosmos, led to the many varying accounts of what we would call 'the universe' known as cosmology and cosmogony. It led also to the exploration of the best way in which to live together in society. There are, of course, many different ways in which people can live in relationship with each other, ranging from hierarchy and authority to sharing and redistribution, and once again we see why there are so many different forms of religion.

The exploration of the meanings and implications of relationship led, as we saw, to the extension of altruism, and to the sense that justice and truth can be realized in society, not just in individual lives. The exploration even led beyond the prophetic voices of protest against injustice (common in many more religions than Judaism) to a realization that the nature of God must necessarily be relational in itself – as, for example, in totally different ways (yet another example of 'differences making a difference'), with Wakan-Taka for the Dakota/Lakota, Trimurti for some Hindus, the Trinity for Christians: 'Ther Treuthe is in Trinitiee and throneth hem alle', as Langland put it long ago (1.133).

Just as important as the exploration of the external world has been the exploration of what it means to be human. These were explorations of what this human entity is, and of what it can experience and become. Even basic human necessities, like breathing, become in many religions a part of that exploration. It is the exploration of what the nineteenth-century American writer Henry Thoreau called (when he argued that there is no object in going round the world to count the cats in Zanzibar) 'the private sea', the streams and oceans of our inner nature (p. 213):

> Is it the source of the Nile, or the Niger, or the Mississippi, or a Northwest Passage around this continent, that we would find? Are these the problems which most concern mankind? . . . Be rather the Mungo Park, the Lewis and Clark and Frobisher, of your own streams and oceans . . . Nay, be a Columbus to whole new continents and worlds within you, opening new channels, not of trade, but

of thought . . . What was the meaning of that South-Sea Exploring Expedition, with all its parade and expense, but an indirect recognition of the fact that there are continents and seas in the moral world to which every man is an isthmus or an inlet, yet unexplored by him, but that it is easier to sail many thousand miles through cold and storm and cannibals, in a government ship, with five hundred men and boys to assist one, than it is to explore the private sea, the Atlantic and Pacific Ocean of one's being alone.

In the so-called 'age of exploration', when Europeans were setting out to discover what to them were new worlds, writers of the time, like Thomas Browne (1605–82), insisted that we should be equally adventurous in our explorations of the worlds within (p. 19):

I could never content my contemplation with those general pieces of wonder, the flux and reflux of the sea, the increase of Nile, the conversion of the needle to the North; and have studied to match and parallel those in the more obvious and neglected pieces of Nature, which without further travel I can do in the Cosmography of my self; we carry with us the wonders that we seek without us: there is all Africa and her prodigies in us; we are that bold and adventurous piece of nature, which he that studies wisely learns in a compendium what others labour at in a divided piece and endless volume.

In point of fact, religions had already for millennia been making those explorations of the inner world. They had led to the discovery of what humans can attain in experiences of immediate, and also of ultimate and transcendent, truth. The, so to speak, landfall of those explorations evoked the languages of Enlightenment, peace, divinization, emptiness, the Buddha-nature; the languages also of worship, adoration, mindfulness, vision and prayer. Those are truths that can be known, not by propositions, but by participation.

Religions offer specific resources, techniques and objectives through which people can explore the furthest possibilities of human experience, ranging from desolation to ecstasy. For some, as for Ruth Pitter, it is a sudden blaze of heaven in an otherwise ordinary world. As she remembered it, 'all was as it had ever been' when suddenly she saw –

> saw all as it would ever be
> in bliss too great to tell.

For Emily Dickinson, it was an exhilaration, a 'divine intoxication', as though a breeze had lifted her like a feather and left her

> in another place
> Whose statement is not found.

The statement cannot be found, nor can the bliss be described, because even for poets words hint but cannot hold – do musicians come closer? Certainly it means that those who have not internalized the constraints that lead to 'another place', a transformed way of being alive, cannot know, let alone put into words, what it is like to be there.

Experience of that kind is far from being the only point or purpose of religions. More fundamentally, they offer resources and constraints to help people in their journey through life; not least when, as so often for so many people, it is pain and burden. In 1862, Berlioz wrote in a letter:

The existence of evil and of suffering, the ferocious madness of the human race, are the insoluble enigma of the world: it has reduced me to the state of grim, despairing resignation which is the scorpion's when surrounded by burning coals. The most I can do is hold myself back from piercing myself with my own sting.

Agonies, as Whitman put it, are our change of garments: 'I am the man, I suffered, I was there.' Nevertheless, each day is one step on a journey that religions convert into quest. That is why Basho began *The Narrow Road to the Deep North* (his account of his search for Enlightenment) with the words, 'Days and months are travellers of eternity. So are the years that pass by.'

That kind of journey is often described and enacted as 'pilgrimage'. It leads to an extraordinary consequence. It is the realization that spiritual pilgrimage leads, not just to discovery, but much more to a profound sense of being discovered – not so much 'discovering God' as being discovered by God. That is why David Burrell once described prayer as 'a response to the unsuspected discovery of my life as a gift by learning how to receive it'. In that sense we are all gifted children. *Prasada* in India, and 'grace' in Christianity, are words that try to catch the unlimited generosity of our creation: 'This is the amiable nature of God,' as William Law put it (p. 72), 'doing nothing but from love, . . . giving nothing but gifts of love, requiring nothing of all creatures but the spirit and fruits of that Love which brought them into being.'

5

On the edge: the boundaries
of religions

Religions, as we have now seen, are socially organized communities in which there are many constraints on belief and behaviour. But constraints are the necessary condition of far greater freedom: the receiving and the internalization of grace, for example, or the attainment of Dhyana, Buddhata, Fana and of so much else – as indeed of 'divine intoxication'.

It is true that constraints can hold people so tightly that the result is a narrow-mindedness in which no question is possible. In the case of religions, it can come to resemble the wooden-headedness of which Barbara Tuchman wrote when she was tracing *The March of Folly* (p. 4):

> Wooden-headedness, the source of self-deception, is a factor that plays a remarkably large role in government. It consists in assessing a situation in terms of preconceived fixed notions while ignoring or rejecting any contrary signs. It is acting according to wish while not allowing oneself to be deflected by the facts. It is epitomised in a historian's statement about Philip II of Spain, the surpassing wooden-head of all sovereigns: 'No experience of the failure of his policy could shake his belief in its essential excellence.'

For the word 'government' in that paragraph substitute the word 'religion', and the point is obvious. The possibility of dialogue within and between religions is made all the more difficult when any of those involved believe that the 'preconceived fixed notions' come from an infallible text or teacher. The constraints are then extremely restrictive. But when, on the other hand, constraints are recognized and understood for what they are, and in particular when they are internalized, they set people free to explore, not just the possibilities of their inner world, but also the nature of their relationship with others.

So far in this book we have seen that the achievements of religions are immense. They have been highly successful in preserving and protecting human life, in giving meaning and purpose to existence, and in sustaining the explorations of both inner and outer worlds. Religions create coherent systems of belief and practice which sustain people in adversity and inspire them into action, and which also have been drawn into the building of ordered societies. That is why religions (each in its own way) are, as much now as in the past, communities of shared imagination and practice in which art, music, drama, poetry and much else have flourished.

It is impossible in a short space like this to describe all the different ways in which religions have done this. But what we can say for certain is that none of it happened by accident. Think back to the earlier sentence when it was pointed out that those people and communities that live perceptively within the limits of constraint are able to survive and flourish: 'If they do so, they build up customs, beliefs, traditions and memories of how and why that has happened, and they certainly take trouble to pass on their accumulated wisdom to their children.'

Because that is so, religions are organized systems that protect the transmission of accumulated knowledge, belief and practice. In summary, therefore, religions are information-processing systems. In the universe, information is fundamental – in the beginning was information – and it does not drift around at random. Information to *be* information (that is, to delimit all the theoretically infinite possibilities into particular outcomes) has to be coded, stored, transmitted and realized, and that means it has to be protected. In that sense, religions can be regarded as systems which do exactly that, coding, protecting, storing and transmitting information in order for it to form within (i.e. inform) human lives.

So whatever else religions are (and they are much else), they are highly organized systems to protect the information that has been identified within the system as essential for successful outcomes in life – with success ranging from the care of an infant to the attainment of Enlightenment or of God.

From this follows an immediate and obvious reason as to why there are many different religions: protective systems of that kind require boundaries, and it is the necessity for boundaries to protect information that leads to distinct religions. We have to draw a line somewhere. The question is: what sort of line should it be? A red line not to be crossed, or a green line, somewhat like a membrane, encouraging interaction and exchange?

The boundaries may be metaphorical: they may, as we saw earlier, be described as the Umma in Islam or the Body of Christ in Christianity. But they may also be literal, a Holy Land, for example, or a sacred space like a mountain or river, or a building like a temple or mosque. It may even be an entire country: the whole of India has been mapped as a place of pilgrimage in the great Indian epic *Mahabharata* (as Bhardwaj has shown), and high-caste Indians are not allowed to travel outside that boundary since, according to the Dharma Sutras (summaries of Dharma: see, e.g., Baudhayana, *Dharmasutra* II.2.2), to do so would lead to loss of caste because the correct rituals and observances become impossible. When Gandhi went to London to study law in 1887, Modh Bania, his own caste, made him an outcaste.

So the boundary conditions of a system of beliefs and practices may be literal or metaphorical or a combination of both. Sixty years ago, Lattimore wrote on why 'the frontier' is important for anthropologists and sociologists in trying to understand the interactions between different communities (p. 374):

> There is need here to touch only lightly and in passing on the various physical kinds of frontier. It is at least necessary to mention, however, that the linear frontier as it is conventionally indicated on a map always proves, when studied on the ground, to be a zone rather than a line. A frontier line separates two jurisdictions; but whether the two communities that are set apart from each other in this way are similar in a general way like France and Italy, or notably dissimilar like India and Tibet, the maximum of difference is to be sought near the centre of gravity of each country and not at the frontier when they meet. A frontier population is marginal.

In the new world of the digital and IT revolution, the lines on a map persist, and they can still be a focus of division, as post-Trump in the case of Mexico and the United States;

and their persistence may well be an expression of the difference between religions, as most obviously in the examples of Kashmir and of Israel.

But traditional boundaries and walls are now increasingly irrelevant or easy to ignore. The dissolution of boundaries makes it much more difficult for religions to monitor and maintain their coherence. They have at least had much practice in doing this in the past. To give only one example, in the case of the Muslim understanding of a single Umma, the Caliphate transcends humanly constructed boundaries – a reason why those who attacked Isis (Da'ish) as being 'neither Islamic nor a state' completely missed the point.

In a less extreme way, it is obvious that whenever people have had to migrate, they have taken their beliefs and practices with them while nevertheless adapting them in ways that enable them to survive and even flourish, as one can see repeatedly in the Jewish diaspora. They may have lost a specific and geographically defined space, but they have been able to take with them their world-picture, including the controlling metaphors along with their beliefs and practices. Thus Mearns describes (pp. 253f.) how Hindus in Malaysia draw on *Mahabharata* to achieve an understanding of their situation outside the boundary of India:

> The Mahabharata epic – the tale of the battle between the forces of disorder and depravity (embodied in the Kauravas) and those of order and integrity (embodied in the Pandavas) – is a classic metaphor in this context in that it presents the setting in which many of the problems of contemporary Indian social life appear mirrored in myth, symbolised in the ancient people and events. The world is ruled by others who do not share the value system and

taken-for-granted understandings of the world which either middle-class or, least of all, working-class Indians demonstrate and reproduce in their religious practice. The principles by which the wider society appears to be structured are beyond the constraints of culture as Indians have created it, yet have to be understood in terms of its evolving form if Indians are to come to terms with them. Chaos reigns, and Indians seek to understand it, mitigate its effects, and ultimately overcome it, through ritual designed to invoke ordered intervention of the deities or by seeking knowledge and self-awareness through contemplation upon the nature of the wider universe of which their society is but a part, and contemplation upon the divine forces which order that universe. In the story of the *Mahabharata* and its re-enactment, both paths are acknowledged and rendered legitimate.

So the boundary conditions of systems of belief and practice may be literal or metaphorical or a combination of both. In different ways, therefore, religions are protective circles. Within them there are webs of organization, belief and practice that people share, but on which they do not always all agree. This sets up a tension and potential conflict *within* those circles which no religion has yet managed to resolve.

It is the tension between, on the one hand, those who believe that the boundaries of their particular circle must be monitored and maintained in order that there can be a sufficient consensus of belief and practice within the circle; and, on the other hand, those who live within the constraints of their particular circle but believe that the purpose of internalizing constraints is to set themselves and other people free to live in the spirit, and not only by the rules, of the religion in question.

The two priorities explain many of the differences between and within religions. They are not dichotomies but, rather, differences of emphasis on a spectrum. At one end are those who believe that they must strengthen the carapace (the word used by Maher earlier on p. 42), the protective shell, in order that they may hand on the received tradition to another generation. At the other end are those who roll back the stone to break free into a new resurrection life. To go back to the example of learning the piano, they internalize the constraints in order to begin to play their own music – to live, in other words, with religious freedom – 'as from the Earth the light Balloon/Asks nothing but release', as Emily Dickinson put it. It is the consummate end of the Zen Oxherding pictures (Bowker, 2010, p. 121):

> Careless of clothes, barefoot, I walk
> the world. Attainment is no longer talk
> but truth. And if this truth you long to see
> see it in this lily, in this tree.

That tension is a major reason why there are differences within religions, and there are many examples of it. We have already seen one in the case of the Salafi and other Muslims. Another is evident in the two Popes alive at the same time in the Vatican: Benedict gave priority to monitoring and protecting the circle in a way which included authority and obedience; Francis does not question the necessity of maintaining the boundary of the circle, but he gives priority to applying the rules to people's lives with discernment of their actual circumstances. After Francis published *Amoris Laetitia* to implement the conclusions of a General Synod on Marriage and the Family, four cardinals asked Francis (in five formal questions, or Dubia, addressed to the Pope) why he was challenging the validity of the existing teaching which is, they said, 'based on Sacred Scripture and on the Tradition of the Church, on the existence of absolute moral norms that prohibit intrinsically evil acts and that are binding without exceptions'.

As a result, as *The Tablet* put it, 'There is an exceptional level of turbulence in the Roman Catholic Church' (see 'Following Peter?'). In response to *Amoris Laetitia* it was reported (*The Times*, 25 September 2017, p. 35) that on 11 August

> more than 60 members of the clergy and lay scholars from around the world signed a formal 'filial correction', a step that has not been taken since the 14th century. Entitled *A Filial Correction Concerning the Propagation of Heresies*, the 25-page letter accuses the Pope of promoting seven heretical propositions.

So to repeat the point, it is not the case that everyone agrees on every detail of the picture of the group or society or religion in which they live. Individuals internalize the constraints into their own structure, history and memories, and as a result there will always be argument and disagreement, even though they may still share the general picture.

To that extent, there is a degree of cognitive consensus, but not of cognitive consent. As we have already seen, there are many different ways of being Hindu, Daoist, Christian, Jewish and so on. Sunni and Shia Muslims share almost everything in common, and yet through the centuries there have been wars between them, as at present in Syria or in Yemen. Catholic and Protestant Christians share much in common, but they remain divided. The constraints available in 'Islam' or in 'Christianity' have been selected and internalized in distinct ways to form differing pictures of the world. This means that within the larger protected circles of 'Islam' or of 'Christianity', there are inner circles which may well insist on the truth of their way of seeing the world and of living in it.

It is in that way that cognitive consensus becomes cognitive bias: a tendency or even a compulsion to see the world in a particular way, and maybe even to regard it as the only true way to do so. When the bias is expressed in organized or group action it can be as ferocious as a mob or as peaceful as a prayer, particularly when it is shared in liturgy or rite. There is thus a powerful connection between cognitive consensus and cognitive bias which clearly affects politics and certainly also affects religions. Once again, the differences make a serious difference.

Many questions then arise. What is the status of people who live in different 'world-pictures'? Can people in a particular circle or inner circle 'opt out' and live in a different picture – can they, for example, convert? Joseph Wolff (with whom we began this journey) converted from Judaism to Catholicism to Anglicanism and ended up as vicar of Isle Brewers in Somerset.

Conversion is not always so easy. People can change from one political party or from one religion to another (or to none), though often in the past there might have been severe penalties, including death, for doing so. Even in the twenty-first century, when the IT revolution has already dissolved so many traditional boundaries, there are societies which monitor and deal severely with those who opt out of the systems of cognitive consensus, whether political or religious. In Islam, the penalty for those who apostatize from Islam is *takfir*, excommunication of those who have become unbelievers (*kafirun*), a penalty that may take the form of execution, as in the saying of Muhammad recorded by alBukhari, 'Whoever changes [*badala*] his *din* [Muslim lifeway], put him to death.'

And then another question: what happens when the boundaries of a particular protected circle come under threat? Threats may be literal or metaphorical. There may be an actual invasion, or even a conquest of territory. Equally, beliefs and practices may be threatened by challenge, contradiction or even mockery. In either case, boundaries need protecting.

Here is a fundamental reason why religions are involved in so many seemingly intransigent conflicts. Beliefs matter. For many people their beliefs are so vital and life-giving that they will always be prepared to die and if necessary to kill in order to defend them and sometimes impose them on others. Religious beliefs are not here today and gone tomorrow, even though many of them have changed greatly through the course of time and some have indeed disappeared. Far more seriously, religious beliefs have been tested and winnowed through time and have been found by countless people to be trustworthy and true.

But *are* they true? What a massive question! It is here that we have to go to the second level of phenomenology (based on the first level of description, the meaning of which was summarized earlier on p. 19), which asks: what is it that has evoked those beliefs and practices that we call 'religious'? And to what do people (or to what might people) appeal as the warrants for their beliefs and actions? What that means I have attempted to show in the book *Why Religions Matter*. Here it is only possible to observe (statistically) that for most people alive today their religion is in truth the way they wish to live; and that consequently for at least some among them their beliefs will be unquestionable. And when beliefs cannot be questioned, the problems of dialogue and of bridging differences are immense. To repeat the observation of Quine, 'The intensity of belief cannot be counted on to reflect its supporting evidence.'

Is it the case, therefore, that people of different religions will always be inclined to 'horsewhip each other tremendously', or indeed to do even worse? Clearly not, because there are many individuals and organizations that are committed to building bridges of understanding between different faith communities.

In the past this has led to many attempts to construct communities and societies in which different beliefs and practices are held together. This has often led to creative change and development, but it has led also to angry dissent and to accusations that the received tradition is being betrayed. Thus, for example, when David captured Jerusalem from the Jebusites, he made it his new capital (with consequences down to the present day) and he adopted novel beliefs in sacral kingship which he found there, leading eventually to belief in the coming Messiah. But at the time, the majority of tribes in the kinship group rejected those innovations in a way that led to the difference between the Samaritans and the Jews.

To give another example, an entirely different exploration of 'sacral kingship' was made in India by the Mugal emperor Akbar (ruled 1556–1605), who used it to try to unify people divided otherwise by religion and caste. As a result, he too faced opposition from other Muslims for subverting Islam, as Moin has summarized the point (pp. 1ff.):

As the epitome of this mode of sacred kingship, he [Akbar] not only established a lasting empire in South Asia of un- rivaled grandeur but also fashioned himself as the spiritual guide of all his subjects regardless of caste or creed. At the height of his reign, Akbar was accused of declaring the end of Islam and the beginning of his own sacred dispensation. There was some substance behind these accusations. Akbar had unveiled a devotional order in which his nobles and officers of all religious and ethnic stripes were encouraged to enroll as disciples. Although not given an official name, this institution of imperial discipleship (*muridi*) became known as the Divine Religion (Din-i Ilahi). It generated an immense controversy – a controversy, it can be said, of global proportions.

Controversy is inevitable, because those living in the neces- sarily protected circle of a particular religion are suspicious (to say the least) of those who seem to be eroding or dis- solving the boundaries. They have a suspicion of what has come to be called 'syncretism', particularly when it is associated with 'indifferentism' taken to mean that it is a matter of indifference to which religion a person belongs.

That is one reason why other attempts to draw different religions together have often led to the formation of new and distinct religions. Sikhs and Bahais are two notable examples of how that happens. But that is not the inevitable result of welcoming diversity with gratitude, and of seek- ing to share inherited treasure without destroying identity. This was the major shift of emphasis between the two great conferences of Christian missionaries at Edinburgh in 1910 and at Jerusalem in 1928 where it was said: 'Our fathers could not bear to think of people dying without Christ; we cannot bear to think of people living without Christ.'

It was that vision which led Darryl Macer from his PhD in molecular biology at Cambridge to the setting up of the Eubios Ethics Institute, in which people from different religions (and none) can address together the many moral and other challenges created in the fast-changing 'new world' of genetics. More recently he has been establishing a global university on 'Sovereign land of Native American tribes' in order to make sure that indigenous peoples can make their contribution (p. 197):

> I have conducted research in around 50 countries of the world to date, and right now am learning more about many indigenous Peoples. My original passion for bioethics as an all-embracing discipline remains from my Cambridge days, and most of what I do I would call bioethics – encompassing the love of life, and the ways people relate to each other, and to other lives and nature.

Sharing of that exemplary kind between people of different religions in order to seek the good of each other and of the world beyond themselves cannot lead to predictable outcomes, nor can it be symmetrical. As I put it when asking (in relation to Tillich's understanding of religions) 'Do differences make a difference?', it is far easier for Christians to receive Buddhist methods of meditation than it is for Buddhists to receive Holy Communion. That does not make sharing impossible, as we have just seen in the case of the Eubios Ethics Institute, or, to take another example, as we can see in the remarkable work of Mark Williams (and now of many others) in taking from Buddhism insights into 'mindfulness' meditation, and applying them to cognitive therapy, and in particular to helping those who have been made vulnerable by depression. This is sharing at the elementary level of our common humanity. As Kabat-Zinn has summarized the relationship (Williams, M., p. x):

> It [mindfulness] is a way of being, rather than merely a good idea or a clever technique, or a passing fad. Indeed, it is thousands of years old and is often spoken of as 'the heart of Buddhist meditation', although its essence, being about attention and awareness, is universal.

Sharing of that kind means that 'dialogue between religions' has to go far beyond words. It demands a sharing in practical ways that go far beyond the already existing and widespread responses to disasters. We have to find ways of exploring together what we can create in, for example, the arts and in music. The arts are a dramatic way in which the shared imaginations of religions can be extended to each other: the arts are, to adapt the phrase of Voltaire, the 'embroidery of imagination on the stuff of nature'. When Daniel Barenboim created the West-Eastern Divan Orchestra with people from different countries, some of which were hostile to each other, he did not regard it as, to use his own words, 'a project for peace': 'The Divan was conceived as a project against ignorance.' A first objective is, to quote from the Introduction to this book, 'to educate ourselves . . . in the dynamics of religious belief and continuity, because whether we like it or not, it is religion which still matters more than anything else to most people alive today'.

Even more to the point, religions can be a major resource in the quest for peace and reconciliation, because each religion in its own way makes that quest a matter of *obligation*. In *Conflict and Reconciliation: The Contribution of Religions* (the result of a three-year project set up and financed by

Gresham College, London) I summarized the point in this way (p. 17):

> Those who regard themselves as belonging to any particular religion are under obligation to put into practice the conditions of adherence, and in all religions the pursuit of reconciliation and peace is a necessary and unequivocal obligation – even though the meanings of reconciliation and peace are differently understood. But in all religions there is a vision of peace which transforms lives that are open to it. Amongst much else, they have had long practice in the pursuit of reconciliation after conflict. William Langland caught it well in his *Piers Plowman* (8.409–15):

> > 'After sharp showers,' said Peace, 'how shining the sun!
> > There's no weather warmer, than after watery clouds,
> > Nor any love that has more delight, nor friendship fonder,
> > Than after war and woe, when Love and Peace are the masters.
> > Never was war in this world, nor wickedness so cruel,
> > But that Love, if he liked, could bring all to laughing,
> > And Peace, through patience, put stop to all perils.'

There is no question, therefore, that within those circles of coherence that we call 'religions' there are obligations to 'seek peace and ensue it', to quote the Prayer Book version of Psalm 34.14. But, as we have seen clearly in this book, there are also obligations to defend (albeit in different ways) the boundary of the circle if it comes under attack.

So there still remains a slightly different question: is it inevitable that there will always be some people who believe, in the protected circle of their own religion, that they are required to defend the boundary even to the point of killing others?

Probably it is inevitable: we live in extremely dangerous times when 'the ferocious madness of the human race' ('la folie furieuse' as Berlioz put it; see the end of Chapter 4) persists, but now with even wider opportunities to express it – even down to the level of hacking and tweets. There are, of course, many constraints that control people into those behaviours, but where religions are concerned, we have to remember that they involve issues of truth and salvation. They cannot be ignored, let alone fudged. Even so, is it possible for people of different religions to live side by side and to work together for the good of each other and of the whole world?

That comes down to the question of how or whether such radically different organizations of belief and practice can relate to each other. There have been three main answers to that question (known in summary as exclusivism, inclusivism and pluralism): only one religion is true to the exclusion of others; while one religion is true, there are elements of that truth in all religions which can therefore be included in the whole; all religions are a plurality of varying ways to seek and to find the one ultimate truth (on these see further Additional text 3).

But maybe the ultimate truth is in itself differentiated, as many believe (as we have seen) of the reality (the aseity) of God. In that case, the ultimate truth of relatedness to God is different from the ultimate truth of Nirvana, a condition beyond relatedness of any kind. Both are equally good in the sense that both are equally to be treasured as attainable and worthwhile goals. But they are different. They are not simply inadequate ways of speaking about the same final state beyond words (though the inadequacy of language happens to be correct). They are pointing to a different outcome. It is the reason why Mark Heim called his book (in which he argued that religious aims *and fulfilments* are various), not *Salvation* but *Salvations*. Perhaps in the end we will discover the real truth of the saying attributed to Jesus that where your treasure is, there will your heart be also.

How, then, might the religions be related to each other in a world where differences make a difference? We have to begin with a recognition that the differences are real and by no means trivial. Throughout this book we have seen how and why those differences have come into being, and we have touched (albeit briefly) on illustrations of what in consequence that has meant. Those illustrations could easily have been multiplied. For example, very little has been said in this book about music and art where the differentiating consequences have been literally audible and visible. In *Why Religions Matter* I drew attention to this in answering the question of how religious art in particular is related to art and the arts in general (p. 202):

> We need to start where so much art, especially from the past, is now collected and secured. We need to walk into an art gallery containing art from the past, and there, hanging on the walls, we are likely to see works of art from different parts of the world. Without much difficulty we will be able to distinguish the different kinds of art. Art from China is recognisably different from African art, or from Indian art, or from European art, or from Aboriginal art, and so on, just as they are easily distinguishable from each other. It is even possible to distinguish Chinese from Japanese art, although that may require a trained eye. Each civilisation has produced its own characteristic art which, in many cases, is instantly recognisable and different from any other.

It is this recognition of *difference* which has led to the extensive and often brilliant exploration of 'otherness' in recent decades, not least in the postmodern world where it appears, in words derived from Latin and Greek, as 'alterity' and 'heterology'. The dilemma is how to respect and value the distinctiveness of 'the other' (in this case in the relation between religions) without assimilating them into a controlling category of explanation. It is the challenge raised by those who reject the category of 'religion' altogether, as we saw at the beginning of this book. There is an immensely helpful (though not always easy) introduction to the issues in Michael Barnes' *Theology and the Dialogue of Religions*, where he poses these questions (p. 64):

> How is it possible to know the other *as other* – without, that is, risking the assimilation of the other to the category of sameness? How, on the other hand, does one avoid positing an otherness which is simply unknowable? My initial response to this dilemma is to seek a different approach to theology of religions: not an a priori theory of inter-faith relations but a reflection on what I am calling the 'negotiation of the middle'.

At the beginning of his book, Barnes, writing as a Christian, summarizes what that 'negotiation of the middle' will mean for him (p. 3):

> Whatever I do, whatever I say, whatever I think, at some point my beliefs, and practices to which they give rise, raise questions about the means which I use in developing relations with others; in brief, questions about power and control and the risk of violence done to the other. The result is a dilemma. How to remain faithfully rooted in my own Christian vision of a time-honoured truth and yet become

open to and respectful of those committed to sometimes
very different beliefs and values?

Those questions cannot be answered unless we first recognize that the differences within and between religions do
indeed have hugely differentiating consequences. But we
need then to recognize also that there is a vital and poten-
tially unifying point of connection among the religions. We
have seen already that that point of connection cannot be
established through large-scale statements or theories about
'human nature'; still less can they be translated into declar-
ations of *universal* rights or laws, even though they can be
put into legal effect through the conventions of political or
social agreement. We cannot, to adapt the phrase just quoted,
take for granted *a priori* theories of inter-human relations.

But what we have also seen earlier in this book is that
there exists a more basic point of connection in the *elementary* conditions of life – of being alive at all. There are
elementary constraints without which life in general, and
human life in particular, is not possible. There is, therefore, at that level a common humanity (to use the word
employed earlier) which offers the opportunity to identify
the non-negotiable conditions of life. On that basis it is
possible to accept certain values as objective, and thus to
begin to construct together a shared future. What we have
to resist at that point is the temptation to build ambitious
vehicles which cannot carry the cargoes of generalization
that are being loaded into them.

At that elementary level of humanity, religions clearly
are varying accounts of a common subject matter. Such
varying accounts are common and familiar in the sciences
where, particularly in evolutionary theory, they are known
as *equivalences*. In Wilson's book, *Does Altruism Exist?*,

there is a lucid summary of what that means, where he gives three examples of how there can be equivalent accounts of the same subject matter (p. 37): 'The examples of accounting methods, perspectives, and languages make it easy to understand how different configurations of thought can be *different but worthy of coexistence*, and how they *can be, but need not be, incommensurate.*' That does not in any way eliminate the challenge of truth. Some theories and paradigms are clearly wrong, as Wilson goes on to say:

> The concept of equivalence does not replace the standard rendering of paradigms. Some configurations of thought are just plain wrong and deserve to be tossed in the dustbin of history. And the good old-fashioned process of hypothesis formation and testing still takes place within each paradigm.

At the level of elementary and common humanity, religious accounts can certainly be understood as equivalences. But the testing of them in terms of truth is by no means straightforward (some might even say 'possible'), because those accounts are not open to the main methods of hypothesis-testing, particularly those of the sciences. But those are not the only methods of assessing truth. In religions, the discernment of truth by participation is equally important (there is a longer discussion of this in *Why Religions Matter*, pp. 19–26): by their fruits you will know them.

It is important, therefore, to remember that what we are seeking here is not a final and comprehensive account of what it means to be human. What we are seeking is a way of answering the challenge of how to live together without feeling that we are under an obligation to 'horsewhip each other tremendously'. The words of Marc Bloch (already quoted on p. 89–90) summarize very well the challenge of diversity and resemblance, applying them here with a slight adjustment to 'religions' rather than 'nations':

> It must, I think, be regarded as inevitable that religions, so different as they are – different in spite of having in common many of their most fundamental ideas – should find it very difficult to know, to understand and, consequently, to love one another.

Love, in all its own immense diversity, is the absolute imperative – and 'love' is not a common word in political discourse. That in itself is not surprising since the word 'love' has many meanings. Love may be a many-splendoured thing, but it is also a many-definitioned word. As Voltaire observed in his *Philosophical Dictionary*, 'There are so many sorts of love that one does not know to whom to address oneself for a definition of it.' The poet Walter de la Mare drew attention to this in his wide-ranging anthology *Love*. Taking the sentence 'he cannot really, then, have loved her', he pointed out how different are the people and circumstances to which that sentence might be applied (pp. xxxivf.):

> With how much of this will any other 'he' or 'she' be likely to concur in regard to those to whom the sentence might be actually applied? To Shelley and Harriet, Swift and Vanessa, let us say; to Bothwell and Mary Stuart; George IV and Perdita; to Paolo and Francesca; to Abélard and Héloise: Thomas and Jane Carlyle; to Christian and his wife; Othello and Desdemona; to Gibbon and the young lady of whom (when on parental advice he had resigned her hand) he said, 'I sighed as a lover, I obeyed as a son.'

In Julian Barnes' novel *The Only Story*, Paul, reflecting on the meaning of love, remembers how he had once listed definitions of love and had found almost all of them inadequate or, to use his own word, bad. He therefore concludes (pp. 205f.) that 'perhaps love could never be captured in a definition; it could only ever be captured in a story' – not only in a story, religions would add, but also in the actions that put their stories into effect.

But 'love' as an attitude and an action does not become impossible simply because it cannot be defined in a simple way. We began this book with the problem of defining the word 'religion', but far from stopping us using the word, it became a challenge to show what we mean by it. The challenge to religions is to find how *together* we can demonstrate the meanings of love. In practice that is already happening in the ways in which people of all religions and none respond to the dystopian realities of life, not only in such major catastrophes as those of earthquake or war, but also in those of 'my neighbour's need'.

That is one side of the paradox of religions: the good that religions can do together for those in need. But there is also the challenge to address *together* the other side of the paradox: the ways in which religions create or contribute to those dystopian realities. This cannot be done in the abstract but only by attending to particular instances; and in order to do that, we would be wise to find some acceptable framework within which Barnes' 'negotiation of the middle' can be undertaken. Without a framework of some kind, we are likely to find that the honesty involved will be too painful for people to stay together.

There is no single framework that must be adopted, but one that has proved helpful is hidden in the acronym SMEALCS. Although that resembles a Gollum-like product of Tolkien's imagination, it is in fact a summary of the way in which the military require orders to be given so that nothing is forgotten or overlooked (see, e.g., *Cadet Training*, II, p. 135). The letters stand for

situation;
mission;
execution;
administration and logistics;
command and signals.

S When people from different religions meet together to seek peace or to address some particular issue, they need first to understand who is talking to whom. In 'Guidelines in Conflict' (in *Why Religions Matter*, pp. 291–5), this is the first of eight practical steps – 'The first is to establish who is actually involved, and who, in the background, is offering support. In a general way people may regard themselves as "Muslims", "Christians", "Hindus", but in practice and in detail they belong to far more specific parts of the whole' – as the earlier discussion in this book of 'circles within circles' has indicated. Once these respective points of view are clearly recognized, it then (usually but not invariably) becomes possible to engage together in understanding what the challenge or the problem or the situation is. All this may in itself be an extremely lengthy process.

M Only then can they decide what they intend to do about it.

E If that is agreed, then the question immediately arises of how they or others will put that intention into effect.

AL That in itself will require a clear understanding of what is needed to support that effort, and how that support will be provided.

CS That will certainly require a careful consideration of intercommunication, of how those involved will keep in touch with each other – much easier now in an IT world.

There is, of course, a major difference between the military use of that acronym and the coming together of religions in this way: there is no one person in charge issuing orders. Instead there is a common attempt to address a problem and do something about it – a colloquy even, more than a dialogue.

Military orders end with the synchronization of watches and the enquiry, 'Any questions?' In colloquy (speaking together with each other) there will be innumerable questions, and the attempt to answer them together will lead to fierce and often hostile debate.

That is why the word 'together' is so important: it is the bridge connecting the different sides of 'otherness' in a way that allows each to participate in the worth and value of the other. Of the differences between 'male' and 'female' the French are inclined to say *Vive la différence*. We can now say that also of religions – and we can do so with a determination, not to pretend that the destructive and damaging consequences of 'the difference' do not continue, but to move beyond them in a practical definition of what the word 'love' actually means.

That is exactly what the remarkable Paolo Dall'Oglio did in Syria when he rebuilt the ruined monastery Deir Mar Musa, with an ecumenical community dedicated to 'negotiating the middle way' between Christians and Muslims. That is why he called his book describing this *Innamorato dell'Islam, Credente in Gesù*. In 2012 he was awarded an Italian Peace Prize, and yet only seven months later he was seized by Isis and, according to Asharq al-Awsat, was executed. Religion hurts.

In their varying iconocosmic pictures of the world, each religion has its own way of identifying the care and compassion (literally, from the Latin, 'the suffering with') for 'the other' that is required of us. In Buddhism, for example, it is obvious in the basic ethics (*sila*), particularly when that was extended in the Mahayana understanding of the *bodhisattva* (the disciple seeking enlightenment) who has mastered the six Perfections and has thus attained *nirvana*. But it remains '*nirvana*-in-this-life' (*sopadisesa-nibbana*) in which a *bodhisattva* seeks to help others. A *bodhisattva* is 'that being' (to quote Paul Williams' summary, p. 49) 'who has taken the vow to be reborn, no matter how many times this may be necessary, in order to attain the highest possible goal, that of Complete and Perfect Buddhahood for the benefit of all sentient beings'. The overriding sense of compassion for all those who are suffering appears very clearly in the *bodhisattva*'s vow: 'However innumerable sentient beings are, I vow to save them! However inexhaustible the defilements are, I vow to extinguish them! However immeasurable the *dharmas* are, I vow to master them. However incomparable enlightenment is, I vow to attain it!'

This 'morality as altruism' (as Keown, p. 40, translates *sattva-artha-kriya-sila*) is, as we saw earlier, fundamental in all religions. In theistic religions, it is derived from the generosity of God in creation, translated and extended into carefulness – seeking always the good of the other wherever it or they are found in the created order. 'God' is yet another word which cannot be exhaustively defined but is known in a relatedness of the One to the other which is expressed in creation and realized in participation. To quote again the words of William Law (p. 68):

> A root set in the finest soil, in the best climate, and blessed with all that the sun and air and rain can do for it, is not in so sure a way of its growth to perfection as every man may be whose spirit aspires after all that which God is ready and infinitely desirous to give him. For the sun meets not the springing bud that stretches towards him with half the certainty as God, the source of all good, communicates himself to the soul that longs to partake of him.

Those extremely different narratives and world-pictures have created correspondingly different consequences in history, society and individual lives. But, as we saw earlier, there is at the elementary level 'a common humanity' on which it is possible to build a recognized and shared moral altruism; and from that may flow common actions freed from suspicion of other motives. Among the religions there will be some for whom the acceptance of 'universals' on particular issues will remain impossible even though they have been enacted internationally. But dissent at that level does not prevent the recognition of an elementary common humanity. Building on that recognition will change the way we work and live together in multifaith and pluralistic societies.

And change is constantly what is needed in the forming of altruistic morality. Fundamentally, it is a change in the ways we relate to those who are other than ourselves. It is exactly as Jane Shaw ended her article on moral imagination (p. 125):

All the reading, all the art, all the liberal humanities curriculums of all the world's universities, make little difference in forging humanitarian communities unless they lead to change – which means that we have to change. The development of a moral imagination requires the capacity to pay careful attention to the other, especially the stranger, and their stories – which may occur via the entry into a story, as encouraged by a parable or a parabolic art form. It also requires the expansion, rather than the narrowing, of our communities. And, finally, it needs something that emerges from these two aspects of story and community but which cannot be contained in any formula – that is the impulse to act with the others' interests at heart rather than our own.

But what if the anger, conflict and intransigence persist in the arguments between and among religions? They are, after all, matters of life and death. Even then – or particularly then – it is important for religious believers to remember that the *final* judgements belong to Karma and to God. It is wise, therefore, to remember G. K. Chesterton's definition of charity as 'a reverent agnosticism towards the complexity of the human soul'. We cannot always be right about everything, and sometimes we really do need to leave the final judgement to God.

The word 'judgement' is a reminder also that religions are themselves accountable, not just as individuals, but also as communities: there is social as well as individual evil, as religions know well in practice. The challenge to religions is to work out how *together* they can do something to confront the harm and damage they have themselves done in the past and all too often are still doing in the present. Only on that basis can they then, *together*, respond effectively to the immense problems that face us all, not least those of climate, population, migration, trade, exploitation, despair, corruption. Even beyond that, it becomes possible, on the basis of a *religious* understanding of responsibility and accountability, for religions to make an entirely new and different contribution to the continuing quest for human rights. As I ended my paper for a UN working party on religions and human rights (p. 173):

> The specific religious contribution to human rights is to define more adequately what it means to be human – the acquisition of our own responsibility and the acceptance that we *are* accountable; and the endeavour to ensure that possibility for all others. When Jefferson contemplated slavery, he once said: 'I tremble sometimes for my country, when I reflect that God is just.' We have even more reason to tremble if we think that God is nothing.

Additional text 1
Treaties in Islam

It is well known that Islam divides the world into two
Houses (sing. *dar*) or domains: the Domain of Islam and
the Domain of War (*harb*) or of the Unbeliever (*kufr*). That
division arises because the Qur'an states that God's intention in creation was for all people to live in unity together.
But historically they have fallen into divisions and conflicts,
pursuing their own rival opinions in defiance of God:

> All people were a single Umma, and God sent the prophets
> with encouragements and warnings, and with them he sent
> down the book with the truth to judge between people in
> matters in which they differed. And no one disputed about
> it except those who were insolent one to another.
>
> (Qur'an 2.209/213)

In Muslim belief, God has repeatedly sent prophets through
whom God's word has been revealed in order to bring people
back to a lifeway (*din*) of obedient relationship with God
(*islam*). Earlier prophets before the time of Muhammad were
either killed or the words have been changed or corrupted
in the subsequent transmission of their message. Thus the
prophets of Judaism and Christianity delivered the same
essential message as did Muhammad, but that message has
been obscured by the introduction of much other (human)
material – as, for example, stories about the prophets, historical narratives, letters and the like.

According to the Qur'an, the world before the time of Muhammad was already divided into two groups: those, known as the People of the Book, who received the revelation even though they subsequently corrupted it; and those who 'set up with their hands images of stone and wood . . . which they called gods and which they worshipped'. Al-Shafi'i (150–204 AH/767–820 CE) wrote in his work on the foundations of Islamic law (1.2):

> God sent Muhammad at a time when people were divided into two groups. The People of the Book were one party, but they had changed some of the laws, and they did not believe in God because they forged falsehood with their own speech, mixing it with the truth that God had revealed to them.

He then quoted Qur'an 3.73: 'Cursed be those who write the book with their own hands and then say, This is from God.' In contrast, 14.1 states: 'A Book we have sent down to you that you may lead all people from darkness to light.' Only through Muhammad has the true and eternal word of God been delivered into the world without human alterations or additions.

The Qur'an is thus the foundation of the life that God intends for all people, and it is the responsibility of those who receive the Qur'an as the eternal message to bring the whole world into that same recognition and acceptance of God: 'When the help of God and the victory comes, and you see a multitude of people entering into the Way (*din*) of God, then rejoice with the praise of your Lord and pray for forgiveness' (sura 110).

Muslims, therefore, are required to bring the whole world into Dar alIslam. They must, in other words, 'make an effort', the underlying meaning of Jihad as we saw earlier on p. 3. The ways in which that aim is to be pursued are controlled by Sharia. Sharia, 'the well-worn path', is the organized working out of what Muslims should do and of how they should act in the world. It is based on the Qur'an and on the way in which that was exemplified in the lives of Muhammad and his companions, the records of which are gathered in traditions known collectively as Hadith.

The working out and applying of what that should mean in the circumstances of life resulted in the different 'schools' of Sharia. They vary in method and detail, but they share in common the belief that to live under Sharia is to live as God intended. It is an obligation for all Muslims to make whatever effort they can to bring the whole world into that same condition. That is why the world must necessarily be divided between those who are within Dar alIslam and those who are not – those who, in other words, are in Dar alHarb. That does not mean that Muslims must engage in *constant* warfare (*harb*) against non-Muslims, though they may have to fight on occasion – for example, when any Muslims are themselves attacked.

There are just over 2 billion Muslims in the world, so they are at the moment in a minority. Muslims, therefore, have to live with non-Muslims, and that has been the case from the earliest days of Islam. From the time of Muhammad onward, treaties have been made with non-Muslims. In ibn Ishaq's *Sira* (Life) of Muhammad, there is a section often referred to as 'the Constitution of Medina', containing treaties with different tribes or groups, and a number of other treaties are gathered in Hadith. Since then there have been many different forms of agreement with other states or governments. Through the course of history, therefore,

Muslims have developed a third domain in the division of the world: the Domain of Treaty or of Truce, Dar al-Sulh or Dar alAdh.

The exact form that each Treaty or Truce has taken has changed greatly in response to the development of the very different political systems that were encountered in the expansion of Islam. Thus the relationship between city-states in the earliest years is very different from the Dar al-Sulh as it was understood and enacted in the Ottoman Empire, where the first codification of Sharia, the Medjella (legal provisions), stressed the importance of reconciliation. As a result, Muslims and non-Muslims were able to live peacefully together. An urgent question at the present time (particularly in pluralistic and multifaith communities) is whether the understanding and implementation of Dar al-Sulh can be developed further into entirely novel circumstances.

At first sight that may not seem likely or even possible. For a start, the four major schools of Sunni Sharia already disagree on how Dar al-Sulh should be put into effect. Even more to the point, existing understandings of Dar al-Sulh focus particularly on the handling of arbitration in commerce and trade, as al-Ramahi's excellent article on *sulh* as a 'crucial part of Islamic arbitration' makes clear.

Even so, the very existence of Dar al-Sulh provides an opportunity for Muslims to develop a new and different way of living in non-Muslim societies – a way that has its roots in Muslim history and understanding. Will it happen? Probably not, because Muslims do not have any centralizing or unifying authority among themselves to engage in such a quest; and also because any such enterprise could only be undertaken in the context of the obligation to bring the whole world into a single Umma or community of Islam.

Any *modus vivendi* must, from a Muslim point of view, retain the *jihad* (effort) to achieve that end. As we have seen repeatedly, it does not have to be by literal warfare. It may be achieved, for example, by working in and through the existing forms of any particular society in what has come to be known as 'civilization jihad'– a policy, in the opinion of Holton and Lopez, pursued by Gülen in Turkey (until stopped by Erdogan) and in the USA where schools and universities have been built to achieve the aim of 'moving in the arteries of the system'. We have seen, at the end of Chapter 2, another example of what 'civilization jihad' can mean in the Trojan Horse enquiry.

But another way of interpreting 'civilization jihad' would be to participate in society with a view to displaying the contribution that Muslims can make to the good of all. Certainly it would remain in the context of Sharia, but it would in itself be a display of the unifying purposes of God in ways that the Qur'an requires. It would mean avoiding options that are *not* obligatory but which, if chosen, demonstrate and emphasize that the differences in Islam from other lifeways do indeed make a difference.

An obvious example of this is the wearing of the veil. The Qur'an requires that women as well as men dress modestly, but the Qur'an does not state the exact way in which that has to be done. Of women it says (33.59) that believing women should cover themselves with their *jilbab*, which means in effect that they must cover themselves in public from the neck to the ankles and below the elbow. The schools of Sharia do not actually prescribe that women must wear a veil. The word *hijab* means basically 'a partition', as between the created order and God. It and other forms of clothing are increasingly becoming, in non-Muslim countries, a partition between the wearer and the rest of society. It is a matter of choice, even though customary styles may in practice be imposed. The choice of a complete covering, including the *niqab* and *burqa*, may well be insisting on a different identity in society, as Juliette Minces points out (p. 51):

> There are two contradictory tendencies. On the one hand, the veil is falling into disuse as a result of women's schooling, work and greater participation in public life. On the other, and in the same countries, some women are ostentatiously taking up the veil for political reasons, as a matter of choice rather than in response to family or social pressures. It symbolises the demand for a more 'moral' economic, political and social life, as prescribed by Islam; a return to the wellsprings of Muslim identity . . .

And there's the problem. In most religions there are visible marks of allegiance and identity, ranging from styles of hair and dress to symbols like the wearing of a cross or the five Ks of Khalsa Sikhs. In general, the legislation in any particular country has to reconcile freedom of belief (where it obtains constitutionally) with the implementation of those beliefs that are socially divisive. Thus Bradney takes as an example the 1989 Employment Act in which 'Sikhs are exempted from any regulation requiring the wearing of safety helmets on construction sites' (p. 6). He then asks:

> If Sikhs are to be exempt should not Rastafarians be given the same exemption? On the basis of various Biblical injunctions such as Leviticus 21.5 Rastafarians believe that hair should not be cut. The consequent dreadlocks are

likely to prevent Rastafarians wearing a safety helmet. Why
are Rastafarians not exempted?

In each religion some, but not all, such requirements are
obligatory. But whether they are an obligation or not, a
divisive problem arises if they are worn in order to emphasize distinction and *difference*. If Muslims living in pluralistic societies wish to contribute actively to the well-being of
those societies, as very many do, then the choice to adhere
to what the Qur'an says, and not to extend it further,
becomes crucial: do we wish to live together in a 'domain
of peace' or not?

Those choices can be made individually and to some extent
collectively under the guidance of imams in mosques. The
challenge for Muslims is to find a way in which together, in
a wider society, they can agree on interpretation and action.
An unusual attempt was made in the UK in 2018 when Qari
Asim, an imam from Leeds, set up a National Council to
issue rulings on controversial issues and to promote what he
called 'a progressive interpretation of Islam'. According to a
report in *The Times* (18 August 2017, p. 17):

It will be the first central religious authority for British
Muslims, delivering edicts on Islamic doctrine and provid-
ing a national voice on social issues. It would state clearly
that 'regressive cultural practices' such as forced marriages
and 'honour' killings have no place in Islam or in British
society . . . Mr Asim said that a board would provide more
authoritative rulings, with imams expected to engage with
the wider community. It could be welcomed as an authoritative Muslim voice by the government and media and
could amplify the efforts of individual mosques that con-
demn extremism but often did not receive national media
coverage.

In the quest to create a domain of peace, the aim of achieving a single Umma remains, but the choice would be made to avoid non-obligatory styles of dress or appearance if they disrupt society at large. It would become, in other words, a demonstration by Muslims of their care for the wider society, and it would thus be in its own way a contribution to that aim of creating a single Umma. The changing history of Dar al-Sulh offers the opportunity to make further changes of that kind in the direction of peaceful coexistence.

That is why Aykol ended his remarkable book, *Islam Without Extremes*, with this plea (pp. 284f.):

> We [Muslims] should rethink what the ultimate goal, and the destiny, of the *umma* should be on this earth. The answer given by the Islamist movement is often a triumphalist one: Islam will simply conquer the whole world; sooner or later, the whole world will be Muslim.
>
> Yet this ambitious rhetoric might be reflecting the ambitions of the people who happen to be Muslims, rather than the intention of the Divine. The Quran, in fact, clearly states that the whole world will *not* be Muslim. 'What has been sent down to you from your Lord is the Truth,' a verse tells the Prophet, 'but most people have no faith' (13.1). Another verse refers not to the lack of faith but the variety of faiths, explaining that this diversity is exactly what God desired for mankind (5.52, my translation):
>
>> And We have sent down the Book [Kitab, revelation] to you with truth, confirming the earlier Book and safeguarding it . . . For each of you we have appointed a law [*sharia*'] and a practice. If God had so willed, God would have made you a single people [Umma], but God wanted to test you concerning that which has come to you. So compete with each other in doing

good. All of you will return to God who will show you
the truth of the matters about which you differ.

The way in which the understanding of the Domain of
Peace has changed greatly in the past and can still do so
now offers the opportunity for all believers, not only to
compete with each other in doing good, but to do so as
friends. The diversities will not go away, and the differences
will continue to make a difference, but in the end the final
judgements will remain with God.

Additional text 2
Christianity and other religions

Towards the end of the last chapter in this book, brief mention was made of three ways in which religions, with all their differences, might be related to each other: exclusivism, inclusivism and pluralism. The terms were effectively summarized by Alan Race in 1983 when he argued unashamedly (to use his own word, p. 104) for pluralism on the grounds that 'the faiths are related around a common purpose, the explanation of "a world of mystery variously symbolized in various ways"'.

A strong argument for pluralism was put forward by John Hick in his Gifford Lectures, published as *An Interpretation of Religion*, and it is the purpose of this Additional text to examine that argument and to consider some objections to it.

Hick accepts that while indeed there are conflicting truth-claims between religions, they can coexist because they are different ways of relating to the ultimate truth and reality, which he calls 'the Real'. The nature of the Real is far beyond the limited power of words to describe. Nevertheless, the immensely varied attempts at characterizing the Real are at least helping people to look in the right direction and to experience a transcendent Other, even though the Real in itself remains necessarily unknowable. Hick's argument is that the experiences which have come to be called 'religious' are sufficiently widespread and common to make it entirely

rational for people to adopt the religious beliefs and practices that relate to their experience.

It is not the case, therefore, that religious belief is (as many
have called it) irrational emotionalism. It is, rather, an
example of reason and emotion working together – the
different understanding of emotion and reason that was
summarized earlier in this book. Why, then, are there so
many different religions? Hick's answer is that the universe
is ambiguous, by which he means that there can be many
different interpretations and understandings of it. There
are, for example, naturalistic interpretations – which, incidentally, can also integrate the rational and the emotional,
as we saw earlier in the case of Feynman.

The ambiguity of the universe arises from the fact that
we can never give a final and exhaustive account of what
the universe is. We can only deal with whatever presents
itself evidentially to our limited perception and discernment. This is an echo of the Kantian distinction between
'the thing in itself' (*Ding an sich*) and the way it appears
to us – hence the distinction between 'the noumenal' and
'the phenomenal' world. As a result, many of our judgements, including those in the natural sciences, turn out
(particularly from the standpoint of later generations) to
be approximate, fallible and corrigible. Nevertheless, many
of those judgements prove to be reliable. That is the case
most obviously with the natural sciences, but it is true also
in its own way in religions.

On this basis, religions can be understood as different but
approximate responses to whatever is truly and ultimately
the case; to whatever is, as Tillich put it, our ultimate concern, to what Hick calls 'the Real'. Consequently, religions
offer different paths and different resources for people to

adopt in order to reach the ultimate goal, the Real. Their descriptions of the Real are expressed in approximate ways, but, so Hick claims, they are pointing to the same truth beyond words. In practice, however, that may lead, not to reconciliation between religions, but to even greater divisions – a criticism that Volf has made (p. 44):

> The trouble is that an unknowable god is an idle god, exalted so high on her throne (or hidden so deep in the foundations of being) that she must have the tribal deities do all the work that every self-respecting god must do. Believing in a God behind all concrete manifestations amounts therefore to not believing in one; each culture ends up worshipping its own tribal deities, which is to say that each ends up, as Paul puts it, 'enslaved to beings that are by nature not gods' (Galatians 4.8).

This means that religions make competitive and competing truth-claims, some of which will turn out to be wrong (particularly when tested against other ways of discerning truth). If it is possible to be religiously right, it must be possible to be religiously wrong.

Nevertheless, in Hick's view, religions in general can be understood to be different ways of pointing and leading people to the Real, and can therefore coexist with each other – the view known as 'pluralism'. In his own words (p. 376), they 'constitute the different conceptions and perceptions of, and responses to, the Real from within the different cultural ways of being human'.

There are many things to be said about that argument, and some are gathered in the book presented to John Hick as a tribute to his work (see Sharma). My own contribution focused on whether the issue in understanding the relationship between Christianity and other religions is the issue that arises from the ambiguity of the universe and the impossibility of giving exhaustive and incorrigible accounts of the Real. That may certainly allow a recognition of the coexistence of religions as alternative paths to 'that of which we cannot speak'. But is it the actual issue?

In trying to answer that question, I began by pointing out that when we think about Christianity in relation to other religions, the first thing we have to recognize is that Christianity began as another religion. It began as Judaism – or, to put it more accurately, it began as one among many attempts at that time to interpret how the revelation and action of God in the past among the Jews should be understood and expressed in the present. If there had been no sufficient reasons for the disentanglement of a different lifeway (Christianity) from the existing ways of being Jewish (often at that time differing very much from each other), then there would be no Christian problem of evaluating its relationship with other religions: there would only be the Jewish problem.

That is a more important point than it probably sounds, because the Judaisms from which Christianity departed were already competitive in relation to other religions in the Roman Empire in terms of truth, and some forms of Judaism at the time were strongly missionary. And it is important for a second reason as well: it has meant that Christianity from the start has incorporated the recognition that God does not deal exclusively with Christians. At the very least God has had dealings with God's own chosen people; and much of the New Testament wrestles with the question of the status of the Jews in relation to God if Jesus is recognized as Christ (i.e. as the *Jewish* Messiah).

What of the wider issue, the status of other claims, outside the boundary of Israel, to a knowledge of God? The engagement of Christians with that question in the early centuries was inevitably bound up with the answers already given to it in Israel. For at the very least, Christians had to recognize that if they understood their own relation to the Jews as being one of a new covenant in relation to the old, then however much the old might be regarded as superseded, it at least affirmed the continuity of God's action from the one to the other. So as Paul particularly emphasized, it could not be held that God's earlier action in relation to the Jews was a mistake. Thus the fact of God's redemptive initiative outside the boundary of Christianity was a matter of (Israel's) history; and since that history contained the unmistakable record of God at work outside the boundary of Israel (and recognized to be so), Christianity inherited an 'inclusive' voice in terms of the freedom of God's action in the world.

But another way of putting the same point is to recognize that God's initiative in repairing the broken relationships which the opening chapters of Genesis summarize (e.g. with God, with the natural order, between husband and wife, between town and country, between nations) led to a succession of covenants. The covenants began with Noah and ended (from the Christian point of view) not with Ezra but with Christ.

But that process (or at least the interpretation of it) carried with it the possibility of an 'exclusive' voice, for which the maintenance of the covenant community is seen to require a strong separation from whatever lies outside the boundary of the covenant process. Paradoxically, that came to include eventually the rise of Christian

Additional text 2

anti-Semitism – the Christian 'war against the Jew' (to quote once more the title of Runes' book). It became an exclusivist attack on the people of the older covenant.

Much earlier, however, Christianity inherited from Judaism a variety of different evaluations of other religions and philosophies, and of the possibility of a true knowledge of God within them, ranging from extreme exclusion to an acceptance that other religions and philosophies are different paths to the same ultimate goal, namely God. Thus *The Letter of Aristeas* (second to first century BCE) based its appeal to Ptolemy for the release of some Jewish captives on that ground *(Ep. Aristeas* 15):

> In the perfection and wealth of your clemency, release those who are held in such miserable bondage, since, as I have been at pains to discover, the God who gave them their law is the God who maintains your kingdom. They worship the same God – the Lord and Creator of the universe – as all other people, as we ourselves, O king, though we call him by different names, such as Zeus or Dis.

The logic of the argument is exactly the logic which was evoked over a great length of time in the biblical period, that if God *is* God, then it is God that God must be. There can only be the one reality to which such language, prayer and sacrifice are addressed. If it is God who brought up the Israelites from Egypt, it is not other-than-God who brings up the Philistines from Caphtor and the Syrians from Kir (Amos 9.7), or 'that bitter and hasty nation' from Babylon (Habakkuk 1.6 RSV), or the Assyrians as a beekeeper gathers his bees (Isaiah 7.18). Thus Aristeas was able to conclude:

> This name was very appropriately bestowed upon God by our first ancestors, in order to signify that the One through

> whom all things are endowed with life and come into being,
> is necessarily the ruler and Lord of the Universe.

But that conclusion, which is by no means uncommon in Jewish writings of the period, did not lead into what would now be referred to as 'indifferentism' – the view that if different religions have simply characterized the one reality in different ways, it is a matter of indifference which religion one chooses, since they are all pointing to the same goal – to what Hick calls the Real.

Indifferentist arguments certainly occurred in the Mediterranean world, but in general the Jews, even those who accepted the logical and biblical argument about God just summarized, remained equally clear that it is still possible to be *mistaken* about that one reality in what one thinks or does in relation to it. Thus when the Jewish historian Josephus (first century CE) wrote *The Antiquities*, part of his purpose was to show that uncertainties and confusions among the Greeks about God can be resolved by attention to Judaism. His argument is not that the Jews worship another God, but that what God *is* is more worthily and clearly established among the Jews:

> At the outset, then, I entreat those who will read these volumes to fix their thoughts on God, and to test whether our lawgiver has had a worthy conception of his nature (*phusis*) and had always assigned to him such actions as befit the power of God, keeping his words concerning God pure of that unseemly mythology current among others.   (*Ant.* 1.14)

So the Jews (or those among them who thought about such things) made exactly that combination of attitudes which (*mutatis mutandis*) has characterized Christian understanding of religions ever since: that if God is God, then claims to a knowledge of God, if they are well grounded, must be knowledge of *God*. But such claims are not necessarily well grounded or unmistaken simply by virtue of the fact that they are made; nor does a claimed knowledge or worship of God under different guises necessarily place the individual or a community in a secure and obedient relationship with God.

It is in this way that Judaism was recognized by the Romans as being competitive and missionary – and indeed divisive – in the empire. As the historian Tacitus (*c.*56 – *c.*120) put it:

> The Jews regard as profane all that we regard as sacred, and at the same time permit what we regard as abhorrent . . . The lowest villains among other peoples abandon the religion of their ancestors and instead are continually sending tribute and donations to Jerusalem – thereby making the Jews even wealthier. (*Hist.* v.4)

Seneca, who was a contemporary of Jesus and Paul, observed (according to Augustine, *de Civ. Dei* vi.11): 'The customs of that most despicable nation [the Jews] have prevailed to such an extent that they have been received throughout the world: the conquered have given their laws to the conquerors.'

Those are obviously the opinions of two men hostile to Judaism. But the attraction of Judaism to many non-Jews in the Mediterranean world was its clear and uncompromising allegiance to God – to the One who is *God*, behind and beyond the multiplicity of cults and philosophies. A Jewish philosopher like Philo (who lived at roughly the same time as Jesus) could accept without hesitation that truth is achieved in Greek philosophy, but it is truth about *God* whose name and nature are known uniquely among the Jews.

In exactly the same way, Christianity accepted that God can be known outside the boundary of the Jewish or Christian communities, but that such knowledge is often perverted and false, not yielding the individual into a saved relationship, the new covenant, with God. So the Apologists could value the worth and beauty of much that had occurred in the classical world, not least in philosophy (so that Plato could be described as 'Moses speaking Greek'), and yet turn with passionate anger against the practices of pagan religion, in idolatry or in mysteries or in public shows. They could recognize *anima naturaliter Christiana*, and yet also insist *spes mea Christus.*

The important point to grasp is that *both* attitudes are rooted in Scripture (in what Christians call the Old Testament as well as in the New). The history of the Christian encounter with other religions is *the history of the working out of emphasis*: should most emphasis be placed on the fact (or what was taken to be the fact) that this is God's creation in which God can be discerned, known and worshipped, or on the fact (or what was taken to be the fact) that in Christ an atonement with God has been effected, as a result of which the confused and conflicting opinions people hold about God have been replaced by the way that can lead to salvation?

Both emphases have drawn on texts for support. Thus in Acts 14.15ff., Barnabas and Paul refused to be acclaimed as gods by the people of Lystra, saying:

> Friends, why are you doing this? We are mortals just like you, and we bring you good news, that you should turn from these worthless things to the living God, who made the heaven and the earth and the sea and all that is in them. In past generations he allowed all the nations to follow their own ways; yet he has not left himself without a witness in doing good – giving you rains from heaven and fruitful seasons, and filling you with food and your hearts with joy.

On a similar basis, Paul argued in Romans 1.18ff. that knowledge of God is perfectly possible, but that people have turned away from the one to whom reason once led them and have lapsed into irrationality: 'though they knew God, they did not honour him as God or give thanks to him, but they became futile in their thinking, and their sense-less minds were darkened' (Romans 1.21). A very similar argument is developed in the speech before the Council of the Areopagus in Athens, in Acts 17.22–31: 'What therefore you worship as unknown, this I proclaim to you.'

On the other side of the emphasis are equally clear state-ments that the irrationality of which Paul wrote is not a trivial error of little consequence: *all*, he insists, 'have sinned and fall short of the glory of God' (Romans 3.23). It is that situation which is addressed by God in Christ, 'reconciling the world to himself' (2 Corinthians 5.19). Consequently, 'No one comes to the Father except through me' (John 14.6).

We have now moved on to specifically Christian ground. Christianity, simply to exist, had to become separated from Judaism, since otherwise it would still be Judaism – or at most a sectarian relic of Judaism like the Dead Sea sect. Why, then, did it eventually (and not without great strug-gle) become separate? And in so far as it did become

separate in a world of sophisticated religious plurality, why did Christianity not exist more modestly as one
possible way of salvation among many? Why, in other
words, did the missionary urgency develop which carried
Christianity across the Mediterranean world – and eventually far beyond – and which asked of people that they
should transplant themselves, through baptism, into the
new resourcefulness of Christ and the Spirit? It is precisely
that urgency and demand which seem to carry the impli-
cation that other religions are inadequate or false. It is that
which has seemed to create the problem of other religions
in relation to Christianity.

When John Hick first addressed this issue, it seemed to
him that the problem could be dissolved by recognizing that
Christianity is not engaged (or should not be engaged) in
enlisting allegiance to *itself*, but rather should be engaged
in promoting an allegiance to *God*, an allegiance which can
already be found in other religions. This change of attitude
is what Hick called 'a Copernican revolution':

> The Copernican revolution in astronomy consisted in
> a transformation in the way in which men understood
> the universe and their own location within it. It involved
> a shift from the dogma that the earth is the centre of the
> revolving universe to the realisation that it is the sun that is
> at the centre, with all the planets, including our own earth,
> moving around it. And the needed Copernican revolution
> in theology involves an equally radical transformation in
> our conception of the universe of faiths and the place of our
> own religion within it. It involves a shift from the dogma that
> Christianity is at the centre to the realisation that it is *God*
> who is at the centre, and that all the religions of mankind,
> including our own, serve and revolve around him.

But that is a very misleading way to state the requirement. We have already seen that Christianity is necessarily committed to that Copernican view (that it is *God* who is at the centre), and it has been committed to this view from the very outset. The issue is not, and never has been, one of *theology*; it has always been one of *soteriology* – of 'salvation': how can men and women, and indeed the whole cosmos, be related to God in a condition which secures them for ever from destruction by sin, evil, death, the devil, or whatever? Of course Hick recognized this. His chapter 'The Copernican Revolution in Theology' begins in exactly that way:

> Christianity has seen itself from the beginning as a way of life and salvation. Our next question is this: Do we regard the Christian way as the only way, so that salvation is not to be found outside it; or do we regard the other great religions of mankind as other ways of life and salvation?

The question needs to be expanded a little, to express the point more clearly, since otherwise it may seem to be implicit in the question that the words 'life' and 'salvation' have the same meaning in all the religions of the world. Once again, we have to remember the warning of Wittgenstein that words do not have a single, agreed meaning that can be transferred from one tradition to another.

So Hick's question would have to be asked in a much more careful way: since other religions are unquestionably ways leading to what they describe in their own terms as the ultimate and desirable goal (though not necessarily described as 'life' or 'salvation'), are those ways efficacious in leading to the same condition that Christians, in their terms and tradition, have characterized as salvation?

Of course, someone asking the question from the stand-point of another religion would not put Christianity in the controlling position, but the focus here is on one example, that of Christianity, of how the salvation claims of one religion are, or might be, related to similar claims in other religions.

Hick's answer is to insist that he *does* know the meaning of the word 'salvation': it is the transformation of a self-centred existence to one that is Reality-centred. As a result, a major part of the way in which the Christian tradition has seen its relationship to other religions (salvation) disappears from sight and is transferred into an issue of theology – namely, whether God is or is not the centre. If what counts as salvation can be isolated and its definition agreed, then methodologically it is straightforward to demonstrate the extent to which all religions exhibit it. That is the method-ology of Hick's *An Interpretation of Religion* (p. 36):

> The great post-axial traditions . . . exhibit in their different ways a soteriological structure which identifies the misery, unreality, triviality and perversity of ordinary human life, affirms an ultimate unity of reality and value in which or in relation to which a limitlessly better quality of existence is possible, and shows the way to realise that radically better possibility. Thus the generic concept of salvation/liberation, which takes a different specific form in each of the great traditions, is that of the transformation of human existence from self-centredness to Reality-centredness.

But is that list of impediments, for which salvation/ enlightenment is the remedy, descriptively realistic for the Christian tradition? Sin, still less aboriginal sin, is not an exact synonym for any of them. And although Hick may be deliberately avoiding religiously loaded terms in order to make the general and universalizing point, it will still remain the case that if the predicament is not described as the traditions (in this case Christianity) see the matter, the remedy may not seem to be applicable either. Thus at the foundation of Buddhism lies the recognition of the human predicament and of the way to deal with it, summarized in the word *dukkha*. *Dukkha* is often translated as 'suffering', but it is more accurately the fact and recognition of transience with the suffering that is necessarily involved in it. The remedy, therefore, lies in the *astangika-marga*, the 'eightfold path' which leads to release from *dukkha*.

Thus it may well be true that 'for fifteen centuries at least the Christian position was that all men . . . must become Christians if they are to be saved'; and perhaps one might wish to call this the Ptolemaic soteriology. But it is a serious confusion to identify this with Ptolemaic theology, as Hick does in, for example, *An Interpretation*, p. 125. For it is obvious that one could have a *Copernican theology* (that God is the centre around which all people and all religions revolve, a position which has always been implicit and usually explicit in Christianity), and combine it with a *Ptolemaic soteriology* (which is also the majority voice in Christianity so far). The issue remains, therefore, not whether God is at the centre, but how people are related to God in terms of salvation.

But even on that issue it is important to note that John Hick made a highly selective use of history, despite his appeal to 'historical relativity'. He illustrated strikingly the ruthless vehemence of the Ptolemaic soteriology, and there is no doubt that he could have illustrated it at even greater length, since it is unquestionably the majority report in Christian history. He then argued that recently (which on p. 123 means 'as long ago as 1854') *modifying epicycles* have been added to the Ptolemaic theory – meaning by 'epicycles' attempts to meet impossibilities in the original theory, not by abandoning the theory, but by adding modifications to it.

Thus Ptolemy himself modified the Aristotelian cosmology, of concentric circles with the earth at the centre, by arguing (to quote Barrett's summary, pp. 12f.) that the five known planets

> move in an epicycle about a point which in turn moved along a circular orbit round the earth; thus did he account for the fact that the planets appeared periodically to reverse the direction of their motion about the earth and to vary in size.

The Copernican revolution was indeed to recognize that the earth is not the stationary centre of the universe but one among other planets orbiting the sun. Even so, as Barrett points out (p. 25), Copernicus had to introduce his own epicycles:

> For Plato and Aristotle the perfection of the circle meant that all celestial orbits must be circles – or combinations of circles – and Copernicus remained so blinkered by that presupposition that he introduced at least as many epicycles as Ptolemy to match the astronomical data.

The epicycles in the soteriological case are such things as the theory of 'anonymous Christians' or a theory of an atonement so objective that salvation is already a fact, so that when, after death, all people are confronted by Christ they will recognize him for what he is.

But what complicates the issue as Hick has presented it is that the 'epicycles', to continue to use his term, are not as recent as 1854. The possibility of people who have lived outside the Christian boundary being saved has been implicit and sometimes explicit in Christianity from the outset, precisely because Christianity attributed to Jesus – and no doubt learned from him, since it is explicit in Judaism – a Copernican theology. Even if God-relatedness (i.e. the covenant) was secured with one people (the Jews) proleptically (i.e. in advance of what will ultimately be the case for the whole of humanity), Jesus came to realize that God-relatedness through faith is open as much to Gentiles as to Jews; and it is to *God*, now characterized as Abba, father, that they are related.

That Christians subsequently emphasized what they believed to be the soteriological implications of Christology, thus creating strong boundary conditions of salvation in relation to Christ, is manifestly true. But what Hick was really calling for is not a Copernican revolution in *theology*, but a questioning of whether the unalleviated Ptolemaic soteriology is correct, in view of the facts that (a) the Copernican theology to which Christianity is committed implies that people outside the Christian boundary can be God-related, and (b) the Ptolemaic soteriology is not, and never has been, the *only* account of salvation in the Christian tradition.

Thus to give only the most obvious example: both Aquinas and Calvin began their great summations of Christian theology (the *Summa Theologica* and the *Institutes*) with the same question and gave it the same answer: can there be a natural knowledge of God? Answer: yes. But where they differ is in the status they give to such knowledge, especially in relation to salvation. Thus for Aquinas such knowledge may in some circumstances be efficacious (thus pointing already to anonymous Christians, long before 1854), whereas for Calvin the most it can do is to point up our culpability in doing nothing of worth on the basis of it.

But that is a soteriological issue, not a theological one (except in the obvious sense that the former always raises issues for the latter). It is certainly not an issue about whether it is God who is at the centre of the universe of faiths. For the obvious point can be made that many planets circulate around the sun, but only one of them is life-sustaining. To put (or keep) God at the centre of the universe of faiths does not of itself determine whether one, or more than one, is life-giving.

Thus the revolution that *may* be called for (in the context of the neo-Darwinian fusion of genetics and selection) is a revolution in the understanding of human nature and of what it would or could mean to be God-related. That is exactly what this book has attempted to indicate. The chapters which apply genetics and the neurosciences to the understanding of why there are religions lead also to new understandings of what it means to be human – understandings to which the sciences and religions contribute together in their different ways. In particular they emphasize the importance of the gene-based (elementary) universals in preparing humans to be what they are in all their immense variety. They include the recognition that human beings are prepared from gene-based programmes for God-recognizing behaviours.

This is very far indeed from genetic determinism. It is the much simpler (oversimple) recognition that the genes build the proteins that build the structure of our bodies, including those of the brain. From this, as we saw earlier, we are prepared for many fundamental behaviours, such as language competence. But the genes do not determine which language we will speak, still less which particular words we will speak. But the gene-prepared competence is a human universal.

In the same way, it is clear that the development of what have come to be called God-recognizing and God-related behaviours is extremely fundamental in the brain (hence the strongly religious nature of young children). It therefore makes obvious neurological sense to say 'Prepared to meet thy God' rather than 'Prepare to meet thy God'. Once again, the genes do not determine exactly what we will do with this competence, but the gene-prepared competence is a human universal.

The truth of that observation (that what people do with that competence is not determined) is evident from the history of religions, since it is obvious that humans have done vastly different things with it. Some are in retrospect (and still may be in the present) absurd, others are cruel and malicious; but others are breathtaking in their beauty, generosity and holiness. They all claim or assume themselves to be God-related, no matter how mistaken some or all of them may be.

So the issue between religions is not whether 'God' is at the centre, except where religions such as those of Buddhists and Jains have completely different understandings of the meanings of the word 'God'. It is whether each or any religion is leading to a secure and ultimate goal beyond time and space.

Thus the Christian issue in relation to other religions will still remain the issue of soteriology. Religions recognize in different ways that there are many thoughts and

actions which evoke a judgement of wrongdoing, even
of evil. Among those thoughts and actions are some that
are a consequence of the unchosen conditions into which
individuals are born, ranging from genetic inheritance to
their own particular family and society. Those unchosen
conditions which have consequence in subsequent life are
described in varying ways in different religions – as, for
example, *karma/kamma* in Asian religions, original sin in
Christianity, *qadr* in Islam.

The question of soteriology is then clear: what needs to
be done if we are to be rescued (or to rescue ourselves)
from the consequences in ourselves and in others of our
unchosen but profoundly wounding inheritance? It is the
question of the young man, 'What must I do to be saved?';
or of another young man, 'What must I do to move beyond
dukkha [the suffering that arises from the fleeting transience of life]?'

The questions are not the same, nor therefore are the
rescues offered. The neo-Darwinian revolution in anthropology cannot judge between them, but it can contribute
much to the discussion. On the one side it gives encouragement to Hick's programme and to pluralism, because
it makes unsurprising the natural human capacity for
God. On the other side it is discouraging to that programme, because it reinforces the realization of religions
worldwide that the composition of many of our abject or
wrong behaviours (and thus of a character which is imbued
with them) precedes our choice or learning. If this latter
is taken seriously (as it was in their different ways, to take
obvious examples, by Krishna, Gautama or Paul), then the
neo-Darwinian revolution in soteriology may have the effect,
not of tending towards indifferentism and/or pluralism,

but rather of emphasizing that the distinctions in religious anthropologies are irreconcilable. That is so, because the *effects* in human lives and character are so differently described that the descriptions of what needs to be done to repair the damage are radically divergent. Here yet again, as we have seen so often in this book, the differences make a real and serious difference.

Additional text 3

Text and interpretation in religions

At various points in this book, and particularly in the section concerned with the way in which in all religions the past enters into the present, it was pointed out that this happens especially through the authority of texts and teachers. Often they claim (or it is claimed about them) that they are revealing truths that cannot be challenged. But the teachings and the texts in the various religions clearly differ greatly in what they say. Those immense differences in both nature and content underlie and reinforce the differences between religions – and that is so no matter how many points of resemblance can be found. There was no space in the book itself to explore how important those differences are. Instead, this Additional text draws on the Introduction to *The Message and the Book: Sacred Texts of the World's Religions*, which summarizes some of the important issues.

The Introduction began with the observation that no one has read all the sacred texts of the world, nor will anyone ever do so. There are simply too many for any individual to read them all. There are at least 100,000 of them, perhaps a quarter of a million, maybe even more, and only a few of them are described in *The Message and the Book*.

Why is the number uncertain? Mainly because it depends on what counts as a 'sacred text', and that in turn depends on what the word 'sacred' means. It is easy enough to go to a Latin dictionary and find out that the word *sacrum* refers to something dedicated to the gods, or even something set apart for the gods in order that they may destroy it. But the original meaning of a word in one language does not tell us what that word has become when it has moved house and taken up residence in another language.

Even so, it may give us a clue. Thus the word 'sacred' may no longer mean 'something dedicated to the gods', but it does often imply that something has been set apart to be revered or respected for particular qualities or associations. The square at Lord's cricket ground is spoken of as 'sacred turf', not because it has been dedicated to the gods, but because it is associated with the highest levels of the game and with the long history of Test Matches, not least against the Australians.

The distinction between 'sacred' and 'profane' in human life and history is so profound that Emile Durkheim (1858–1917), who is regarded by many as 'the father of social science', took it to be the essence of religion. As he wrote in *The Elementary Forms of the Religious Life* (pp. 52, 62):

> All known religious beliefs, whether simple or complex, present one common characteristic: they presuppose a classification of all things, real and ideal, of which men think, into two classes or opposed groups, generally designated by two distinct terms which are translated well enough by the words *profane* and *sacred* . . . A religion is a unified system of beliefs and practices relative to sacred things, that is to say, things set apart and forbidden.

To call a text 'sacred', therefore, implies that it is different in some way from other more ordinary texts. But in what way – or rather, in what ways, since there is no single or simple criterion of distinction or difference?

The most obvious way in which a text might be called sacred lies in the claim that it does not come from a human author, or at least not from a human author alone. Many texts are believed to come from God (or from some equivalent external source), because God has either written them or inspired people to speak or write them. The ways in which the religions in question believe that God has done this are extremely varied – another example of 'differences making a difference'. What many of them have in common is the belief that a text is sacred if it is Revelation and if it is inspired. Bible, Qur'an and Vedas are examples, but they are very different from each other in both content and form.

By no means all the texts regarded as 'sacred' are in the category of Revelation. A large number of texts are revered and set apart because they contain teaching that leads to Enlightenment. The 'sacred texts' of Buddhists or of Jains, for example, are not revealed by God, but they are set apart and distinguished because in the case of Buddhists they contain the Teaching of the Buddha, the one who has himself attained Enlightenment and can therefore show the way, or because in the case of Jains they contain the Teaching of 'the Ford-makers', the Tirthankaras, who can therefore be trusted as guides.

So how do we know which are the texts of Revelation or of Teaching? Where Revelation is concerned, it will already be obvious that texts cannot be picked out as revealed on the ground that they contain some agreed and obvious characteristic. Texts do not come into the world stamped with a seal saying 'revealed', 'sacred' or 'inspired'. To say that a text is 'sacred' is a human judgement.

There are many reasons why in the past that judgement has been made about particular texts, whether of

Revelation or of Teaching. The judgement often relates to origin and content. In other words, the judgement is made on the basis of how a text is believed to have come into being, or on the basis of what it contains. For Buddhists, for example, a basic test is whether the text in question helps the person using it to attain the goal of Enlightenment.

Fundamental, however, to that judgement is the recognition or acceptance that some particular texts or group of texts have authority. The word 'authority' is derived from the Latin *auctoritas*, which in turn is related to *auctor*, 'author'. If, for example, God is believed to be the *auctor* of creation, the unproduced Producer of all that is, then God has authority over what has been brought into being. If God, in conjunction with human agency, is believed to be the *auctor* of some particular words, then those words have authority. Beyond that, sacred texts, by having authority, may become the author (or at least joint-author) of the stories that people tell through their lives and histories.

What that means in effect is that sacred texts offer to people warrants and justification for what they think, say and do. The appeal to a sacred text for warrant and justification may be direct and literal, or it may be mediated through interpretation and exegesis, but in either case it is believed that the words should guide or control or inspire the lives of those who read or hear them. The words are then translated into the lives of individuals and into the organization of families and societies.

Because sacred texts have authority, people go to them for an immense variety of reasons, ranging from a direct encounter with God or an immediate experience of Enlightenment, to a need for reassurance, guidance or inspiration. Some may go for far more elementary reasons – to predict the future, for example, or to find a wife.

They also go to texts in extremely varied ways and with very different expectations. As a result, it is possible for people to read the same sacred text and find in it entirely different and often conflicting meanings. It is exactly as William Blake observed in 'The Everlasting Gospel' (α):

> The vision of Christ that thou dost see
> Is my vision's greatest enemy ...
> Thine is the friend of all mankind,
> Mine speaks in parables to the blind;
> Thine loves the same world that mine hates,
> Thy Heaven doors are my Hell gates ...
> Both read the bible day and night;
> But thou read'st black where I read white.

The consequence has been not only disagreement but such contest and anger that it can lead to religious wars. The point is that there is no single 'meaning' of a text waiting to be found and accepted by all people, and that is true despite the way authority figures in religions often attempt to impose an official 'meaning' on a text. In fact, and in contrast to that, texts offer rich opportunities of meaning and interpretation.

There are of course limits of possibility set by the text itself – not *all* meanings are possible! Nevertheless, the experience of reading or hearing a sacred text is a two-way interaction: the text offers to readers or listeners challenge and opportunity, but readers and listeners discern in the text the meanings that connect with their own experience and biography – not necessarily in an isolated way, since the hearing and reading of texts often take place in communities.

The fundamental question (and it is indeed the question of fundamentalism in the religious understanding of sacred texts) is whether the text *dictates* its meaning to the reader, or whether the reader *discerns* within the text meanings that have authority but are not necessarily fixed or certain. Dictation theories of meaning allow the text to move from page to person in a direct way, as though the unchanging meaning of the text is already contained within it and can therefore be applied directly to any circumstance or person without the intervention of much, if any, interpretation.

To give an example, it was a dictation understanding of meaning that led to the three Strode children (Matthew, 6, Pepper, 7, and Duffey, 11) being repeatedly suspended from their school in McDowell County, North Carolina, for preaching in the playground. They were suspended (according to the *Philadelphia Inquirer*, 4 September 1988, p. 19a) for

> hurling biblical invective – including references to 'whoremongers,' 'fornicators' and 'adulterers' – at their teachers ... 'I never called anybody anything,' said Duffey of his preaching. 'I just quoted the verse, "Marriage is honorable in all and the bed undefiled, but whoremongers and adulterers God will judge," and I guess they took that personally.'

In contrast to the dictation of meaning is the discernment of meaning in what is known as 'hermeneutics' (the shared discipline of interpreting and understanding texts). The 'hermeneutic of opportunity' emphasizes that no text has a single, unequivocal 'meaning': the text still has authority, but its possible meanings have to be discerned. Those meanings may be contested, and certainly they may change and develop in the course of time, or even in the course of a single lifetime.

Here is an obvious and continuing reason why there are such deep divisions within and between religions: there is no agreement on what counts as a legitimate method of interpretation. There is no agreement, in other words, on hermeneutics. As we saw in the case of the Constitution of the United States, there is no dispute about the authority of the Constitution. The Originalists are divided on the question of interpretation: should one go back to the original text and apply its meaning as exactly as the Founding Fathers intended, or should one take the intention and apply it with flexibility to changing circumstances? The massive differences in consequence can be seen repeatedly in the judgements of the Supreme Court.

Mutatis mutandis, the same issue divides interpretation of authoritative texts in the religious world, and once again the consequences can be massive. One need only think, for example, of the deeply divisive debates about the interpretation of Bible or of Qur'an in relation to homosexuality.

Some religions, it is true, have tried to draw up principles of interpretation in the hope that there will be an agreement on hermeneutics. An obvious example lies in the 7 and 13 rules (*middoth*) of Hillel and Ishmael in early rabbinic Judaism (they are listed in my *Targums and Rabbinic Literature*, Appendix II). At the opposite extreme is a proliferation of different kinds of interpretation drawing on the postmodern belief that the meaning of the text is always influenced, or even determined, by the context and perspective of the interpreter: there is no single 'meaning' of the original text. An example of the many different kinds of interpretation that can then arise can be seen in the programme of a colloquium in 2017 on 'reading the Gospel of Mark in the 21st century'. Geert Van Oyen introduced the programme by summarizing the developments in hermeneutics in recent years:

> In the decades after the 1971 Colloquium on the Gospel of Mark which focused on Tradition and Redaction, scholarship has witnessed a proliferation of approaches. Alongside historical-critical methods narrative criticism and other readings have found a place in scholarship (feminist reading, reader response criticism, rhetorical analysis, post-colonial interpretations, performance criticism, reception history, social-scientific studies, Gospel and art). This wide range of methods calls for a fresh state of the art of research on Mark . . . The general issue of the relationship between meaning and method leads to more specific research topics. We think, for instance, of the role of the real reader in interpretation, the choice of a specific hermeneutical model, the integration of different disciplines, the function of intra- and intertextual references, the interrelationships of the canonical Gospels or the challenge how to disseminate scholarly information.

It is obvious, therefore, that the interpretation of texts is extremely complicated. Even specialists in hermeneutics acknowledge its complexity. To give only one example, Suleiman wrote (p. 6):

> Audience-oriented criticism is not one field but many, not a single widely trodden path but a multiplicity of crisscrossing, often divergent tracks that cover a vast area of the critical landscape in a pattern whose complexity dismays the brave and confounds the faint of heart.

So the meaning of sacred texts, whether of Revelation or of Teaching, is not immutably fixed or agreed. There is no single 'meaning' of a text. The meanings are created in the interaction between texts and readers, leading to great diversity in the lives of those who hear or read them.

The fact that there are no universally agreed methods of interpretation, let alone of the meaning of any particular text, reinforces greatly the differences between and within religions. That is why the Conclusion of *The Message and the Book* is called 'Sacred Texts and the Burning of Books', asking and answering the question (p. 354), 'Why have sacred texts so often been thrown on the fires of hatred, not least by religious believers?' There also the appeal is made that, as a contribution to a better relationship between religions, we should on occasion engage together in the reading of each other's texts:

> What is clear, therefore, is that the burning of Books will continue, at least metaphorically and often literally, unless we can begin to *share together* an understanding of what methods of exegesis and interpretation are legitimate and permissible in each tradition. If we can then participate *together* in that work of interpretation and application, there is a better chance that we can also work together effectively to change ourselves and the world in the direction of generosity and peace.

What remains problematic is the fact that in the interaction between religions, the participants have to read most texts in translation. But no translation, we are often told, can ever adequately represent the original text. As the familiar Italian saying has it, *Traduttore traditore*, 'Translators are traitors.' The endeavour to translate is always frustrated, because there is no single, original meaning to be found: there are only the possibilities of meaning, some of which may be more probable than others, but none of which can be exclusively exact. All translations are interpretations and are always open to correction.

That is true, but it does not make translations worthless. In fact the world owes to translators an immense debt of gratitude. They are the true pioneers of globalization since without their work we would remain isolated from each other and diminished. However approximate translations may be, it is possible to enter through them into the new and other worlds created by far-ranging explorations of the human spirit and imagination, and preserved now in sacred texts.

Through these sacred texts, therefore, there can be a conversation with the past that entirely transforms the present – and that can happen even in translation. To give an example: Hugh Kenner in *The Pound Era* analysed the way in which Ezra Pound's engagement with Chinese poetry transformed the nature of poetry itself. He pointed out how much Pound relied on Mathews' *Chinese-English Dictionary* and on Karlgren's painstaking attempt to supply a word-by-word representation of Chinese words in English. It enabled Pound, not to translate the Chinese, but to write his own poetry in which he endeavoured to catch the atmosphere (*feng*) of the original. Kenner wrote (p. 521):

> We are deep in the whispering forest of all traditional poetries . . . where the very words to which millions of minds respond have helped form the minds that respond to them. You and I and Ezra Pound are attending to them for the first time, with Mathews' and Karlgren's help. Follow Pound, put 'East Wind' for your title, write

> Soft wind of the vale
> that brings the turning rain,

and you stir the whispers of a different forest, the one in which English sensibilities have learned to feel that 'vale' is less topographical than 'valley' . . . where moreover soft winds when they blow through very short lines of verse animate a lyric tradition so nearly anonymous that it is rather an air in the mind than a cluster of examples . . . For no more than a Christian can disassociate lying down by still waters from the Good Shepherd, can a Chinese be expected to isolate *feng*, the wind, in these Odes, from generations of moral commentary. There is no way to translate all this.

The first marks cut with consistency into clay or scratched on oracle bones in China cannot be deciphered as though we can know what they 'mean', and the same is true of all those many subsequent words written or printed in texts. We can nevertheless respond to them and we may on occasion be moved by them into such a transformed awareness that we are led into the creation of our own new meaning. We can indeed discover truth. And that is the invitation of the sacred texts of the world:

> Deliberated marks
> cut first in clay
> then penned oblique and cursive
> to convey
> the enigma of intelligence:
> communication from a mind
> otherwise extinct and gone,
> a letter from the lost, unsigned
> and open to interpretation.

And yet . . .
one touch enough
to startle sleepiness
from a half open eye into a rough
intelligence: moved by meaning
perhaps even not meant: but see!
a sharp alert, a resurrection life,
idiosyncrasy.

It is now our turn to hear the whispers of those different forests and to touch for ourselves the texts of time. In that way the differences between religions will remain, but we will have a better understanding of them, and a better chance of working together for the good of all.

Bibliography

al-Ramahi, A., 'Sulh: A Crucial Part of Islamic Arbitration', London School of Economics Law, Society and Economy Working Papers, 12, 2008: <http://ssrn.com/abstract=1153659>.

al-Shafiʻi: see Khadduri.

Allott, P., 'Europe and the Idea of the Transcendental: Human Rights and Other Imagined Entities', *Annali di Scienze Religiose*, 2017, pp. 51–71.

American Anthropological Association, 'Statement on Human Rights', *American Anthropologist*, 1947, pp. 539–43.

Andersen, M., 'Predictive Coding in Agency Detection', *Religion, Brain and Behaviour*, 2017, pp. 1–20: <https://doi.org/10.1080/2153599X.2017.1387170>.

—— *et al.*, 'Agency Detection in Predictive Minds: A Virtual Reality Study', *Religion, Brain and Behaviour*, 2017, pp. 1–13: <https://doi.org/10.1080/2153599X.2017.1378709>.

Aykol, M., *Islam Without Extremes: A Muslim Case for Liberty*, New York, Norton, 2011.

Barenboim, D.: see Vulliamy.

Barnes, J., *The Only Story*, London, Jonathan Cape, 2018.

Barnes, M., *Theology and the Dialogue of Religions*, Cambridge, Cambridge University Press, 2002.

Barrett, P., *Science and Theology since Copernicus: The Search for Understanding*, London, T. & T. Clark, 2004.

Basho, Matsuo: see Nobuyuki.

Bassett, A. T., *Gladstone's Speeches: Descriptive Index and Bibliography*, London, 1916.

Baudhayana: see Olivelle.

Bergunder, M., 'Comparison in the Maelstrom of Historicity: A Postcolonial Perspective on Comparative Religion', in Schmidt-Leukel, *qv*.

Berlioz, H., letter to Carolyne von Sayn-Wittgenstein, 22 July 1862, Hopkinson Berlioz Collection, National Library of Scotland.

Beversluis, J., *A Source Book for Earth's Community of Religions*, Grand Rapids, CoNexus Press, 1996.

Bhardwaj, S. M., *Hindu Places of Pilgrimage in India: A Study in Cultural Geography*, Berkeley, University of California Press, 1983.

Blackstone, W., *Commentaries on the Laws of England*, Oxford, 1768–9.

Blake, W., 'The Everlasting Gospel', in G. Keynes, ed., *Blake: Complete Writings*, London, Oxford University Press, 1972, pp. 748–59.

Bloch, M., *Strange Defeat: A Statement of Evidence Written in 1940*, London/New York, W. W. Norton & Co., 1999.

Boë L. J. *et al.*, 'Evidence of a Vocalic Proto-System in the Baboon (*Papio papio*) Suggests Pre-Hominin Speech Precursors', 2017, *PLOS ONE* 12(1): e0169321: <https://doi.org/10.1371/journal.pone.0169321>.

Borger, R. and Cioffi, F., *Explanation in the Behavioural Sciences: Confrontations*, Cambridge, Cambridge University Press, 1970.

Bowker, J. W., *The Targums and Rabbinic Literature: An Introduction to Jewish Interpretations of Scripture*, Cambridge, Cambridge University Press, 1969.

——, 'Can Differences Make a Difference? A Comment on Tillich's Proposals for Dialogue between Religions', *Journal of Theological Studies*, 1973, pp. 158–88.

——, *The Meanings of Death*, Cambridge, Cambridge University Press, 1991.

——, *Is God a Virus? Genes, Culture and Religion*, London, SPCK, 1995.

——, ed., *The Oxford Dictionary of World Religions*, Oxford, Oxford University Press, 1997.

——, 'The Religious Understanding of Human Rights and Racism', in Honoré, *qv*, pp. 153–73.

——, *World Religions*, London, Dorling Kindersley, 2003.

——, *What Muslims Believe*, Oxford, Oneworld, 2009.

——, *Before the Ending of the Day: Life and Love, Death and Redemption*, Toronto, Key Publishing, 2010.

——, *The Message and the Book: Sacred Texts of the World's Religions*, London, Atlantic Books, 2011.

——, *God: A Very Short Introduction*, Oxford, Oxford University Press, 2014.

——, *Beliefs that Changed the World*, London, Quercus, 2015.

——, *Why Religions Matter*, Cambridge, Cambridge University Press, 2015.

Bradney, A., *Religions, Rights and Laws*, Leicester, Leicester University Press, 1993.

Browne, T., *The Voyce of the World: Selected Writings of Sir Thomas Browne*, London, Faber, 1968.

Burrell, D., 'Prayer as the Language of the Soul', *Soundings*, 54, 1971, pp. 388–400.

Cadet Training, London, War Office, 1956.

Calow, P., *Biological Machines: A Cybernetics Approach to Life*, London, Arnold, 1976.

Cartwright, N., 'Simplicity', in Honderich, *qv.*

Chryssides, G. D., 'Buddhism and Conscience', in Hoose, *qv*, pp. 176–99.

Chupp, T., and Swanson, S., 'Medical Imaging with Laser-polarised Noble Gases', *Advances in Atomic, Molecular and Optical Physics*, 45, 2001, pp. 41–98.

Clark, A., *Surfing Uncertainty: Prediction, Action, and the Embodied Mind*, Oxford, Oxford University Press, 2016.

Cohen, A., and Stern, R., *Thinking about the Emotions: A Philosophical History*, Oxford, Oxford University Press, 2017.

Colville, J., *The Fringes of Power: Downing Street Diaries, 1939 – October 1941*, London, Hodder & Stoughton, 1986.

Crick, F., *The Astonishing Hypothesis: The Scientific Search for the Soul*, London, Touchstone, 1995.

Crockett, M. J., *et al.*, 'Moral Transgressions Corrupt Neural Representations of Value', *Nature Neuroscience*, 2017: doi:10.1038/nn.4557.

Dall'Oglio, P., *Innamorato dell'Islam, Credente in Gesù*, Milan, Jaca Book, 2011.

Darwin, C., letter to Lyell, 28 September 1860, Darwin Correspondence Project, No. 2931.

Dawkins, R., *The Selfish Gene*, Oxford, Oxford University Press, 1976.

Deeley, P. Q., 'The Religious Brain: Turning Ideas into Convictions', *Anthropology and Medicine*, 2, 2004, pp. 245–67.

Dennett, D., *Consciousness Explained*, Boston, Little, Brown, 1991.

Deutsch, D., and Marletto, C., 'Constructor Theory of Information', *Proceedings of the Royal Society*, 471, 2016.

Dharmasutras: see Olivelle.

Dickinson, E., *The Complete Poems of Emily Dickinson*, Boston, Little, Brown, 1924.

Doi, A. R. I., *Sharia: The Islamic Law*, London, Ta Ha, 1997.

Durkheim, E., *The Elementary Forms of the Religious Life* (1912), tr. J. W. Swain, New York, Collier, 1961.

Edwards, M. J., Adams, R. A., *et al.*, 'A Bayesian Account of "Hysteria"', *Brain: A Journal of Neurology*, 135, 2012, pp. 3495–512.

Engle, K., 'From Skepticism to Embrace: Human Rights and the American Anthropological Association from 1947–1999', *Human Rights Quarterly*, 23, 2001, pp. 536–59.

Evans, R. A., and Evans, A. F., *Human Rights: A Dialogue between the First and Third Worlds*, Maryknoll, Orbis Books, 1983.

Feldman Barrett, L., *How Emotions Are Made: The Secret Life of the Brain*, London, Macmillan, 2017.

Feynman, M., *Perfectly Reasonable Deviations from the Beaten Track: The Letters of Richard P. Feynman*, New York, Basic Books, 2005.

'Following Peter? *Amoris Laetitia* Special', *The Tablet*, 27 February 2017.

Fox, M. A., *The Case for Animal Experimentation: An Evolutionary and Ethical Perspective*, Berkeley, University of California Press, 1986.

Frayn, M., *Headlong*, London, Faber, 2012.

Gates, B., *Freedom and Authority in Religions and Religious Education*, London, Cassell, 1996.

Gladstone, W. E.: see Bassett.

Goetz, S., and Taliaferro, C., *A Brief History of the Soul*, Oxford, Wiley-Blackwell, 2011.

Gouldner, A. W., *The Coming Crisis of Western Sociology*, London, Heinemann, 1971.

Greene, J., *Moral Tribes: Emotion, Reason, and the Gap between Us and Them*, London, Atlantic Books, 2014.

The Guardian, 'Trojan Horse': see 'Trojan Horse'.

Hardy, T., *Jude the Obscure*, New York, Harper, 1896.

Harvey, A. (2012), *Is Scripture Still Holy? Coming of Age with the New Testament*, Grand Rapids, Eerdmans, 2012.

Hathaway, O., and Shapiro, S., *The Internationalists*, New York, Simon & Schuster, 2017.

Heim, M., *Salvations: Truth and Difference in Religion*, Maryknoll, Orbis Books, 1997.

Hengel, M., *Judaism and Hellenism: Studies in Their Encounter in Palestine during the Early Hellenistic Period*, London, SCM Press, 1974.

Hick, J., *An Interpretation of Religion*, London, Macmillan, 1989.

Holton, C., and Lopez, C., *Gulen and the Gulenist Movement: Turkey's Islamic Supremacist Cult and Its Contributions to the Civilization Jihad*, Washington, Center for Security Policy Press, 2015.

Honderich, T., *The Oxford Companion to Philosophy*, Oxford, Oxford University Press, 1995.

Honoré, D. D., *Trevor Huddleston: Essays on His Life and Work*, Oxford, Oxford University Press, 1998.

Hoose, J., *Conscience in World Religions*, Notre Dame, University of Notre Dame, 1999.

Howard, D., *Being Human in Islam: The Impact of the Evolutionary Worldview*, London, Routledge, 2011.

Huckfeldt, R., Johnson, P. V., and Sprague, J., *Political Disagreement: The Survival of Diverse Opinions within*

Communication Networks, Cambridge, Cambridge University Press, 2004.

Hunter, J. D., 'Fundamentalism: An Introduction to a General Theory', in Silberstein, *qv*, pp. 27–41.

Kabat-Zinn: see Williams, M.

Karlgren, B., *Analytic Dictionary of Chinese and Sino-Japanese*, Paris, Guenther, 1923.

Kenner, H., *The Pound Era*, London, Pimlico, 1991.

Keown, D., *The Nature of Buddhist Ethics*, London, Macmillan, 1992.

Khadduri, M., *War and Peace in the Law of Islam*, Baltimore, Johns Hopkins Press, 1955.

——, *al-Shafi'i's Risala: Treatise on the Foundations of Islamic Jurisprudence*, Cambridge, Islamic Texts Society, 1961.

——, *The Islamic Law of Nations: Shaybani's Siyar*, Baltimore, Johns Hopkins Press, 1966.

Kircher, T., and David, A., *The Self in Neuroscience and Psychiatry*, Cambridge, Cambridge University Press, 2003.

Langland, W., *Piers Plowman*, tr. Terence Tiller, Hertfordshire, Wordsworth Editions, 1999.

Lattimore, O. D., 'The Frontier in History', in Manners, *qv*, pp. 374–86.

Law, W., *Selected Mystical Writings of William Law*, ed. S. Hobhouse, London, Rockliff, 1938.

Lemcio, E. E., *A Man of Many Parts*, Cambridge, Clarke & Co., 2015.

Leonard, M. K., *et al.*, 'Perceptual Restoration of Masked Speech in Human Cortex', *Nature Communications*, 7, 2016: doi:10.1038/ncomms13619.

Letokhov, V., *Laser Control of Atoms and Molecules*, Oxford, Oxford University Press, 2007.

Liu, G., Karlan, P. S., and Schroeder, C. H., *Keeping Faith with the Constitution*, Oxford, Oxford University Press, 2010.

Ludvik, C., *Hanuman in the Ramayana of Valmiki and the Ramacaritamanasa of Tulsi Dasa*, Delhi, Motilal Banarsidass, 1994.

Macer, D., 'God, Life, Love, and Religions among Indigenous Peoples of the World', in Lemcio, *qv*, pp. 196–211.

MacLaughlin, J., *Is One Religion as Good as Another?*, London, Burns & Oates, 1891.

Maclean, F., *A Person from England*, London, Jonathan Cape, 1958.

Maher, S., *Salafi-Jihadism: The History of an Idea*, London, Hurst, 2016.

Manners, R. A., and Kaplan, D., *Theory in Anthropology: A Source Book*, London, Routledge, 1969.

Mare, W. de la, *Love*, London, Faber, 1943.

Mayo, O., *Natural Selection and Its Constraints*, London, Academic Press, 1983.

Mayr, E., 'Cause and Effect in Biology', *Science*, 134, 1961, pp. 1501–6.

Mearns, D. J., *Shiva's Other Children: Religion and Social Identity amongst Overseas Indians*, New Delhi, Sage, 1995.

Minces, J., *The House of Obedience: Women in Arab Society*, London, Zed Press, 1980.

Moin, A. A., *The Millennial Sovereign: Sacred Kingship and Sainthood in Islam*, New York, Columbia University Press, 2014.

Newman, J. H., *Parochial and Plain Sermons*, vol. V, 2nd edn, London, 1842.

———, 'Biglietto Speech', *The Angelus*, December 2010.

Nobuyuki, Yuasa, *Basho: The Narrow Road to the North and Other Travel Sketches*, London, Penguin, 1996.

Olivelle, P., *The Dharmasutras: The Law Codes of Apastamba, Gautama, Baudhayana, and Vasistha*, Delhi, Motilal Banarsidass, 2000.

Ostler, N., *Empires of the Word: A Language History of the World*, London, Folio Society, 2010.

Oyama, S., *The Ontogeny of Information*, 2nd edn, Durham, Duke University Press, 2000.

Palmer, H. P., *Joseph Wolff: His Romantic Life and Travels*, London, Heath Cranton, 1935.

Pitter, R., *Collected Poems*, London, Enitharmon, 1997.

Purcell, E. A., *Originalism, Federalism, and the American Constitutional Enterprise: A Historical Inquiry*, New Haven, Yale University Press, 2007.

Quine, W. V., and Ullian, J. S., *The Web of Belief*, New York, Random House, 1970.

Race, A., *Christians and Religious Pluralism: Patterns in the Christian Theology of Religions*, London, SCM Press, 1983.

Radhakrishnan, S., *East and West, the End of Their Separation*, New York, Harper & Brothers, 1956.

Regan, T., *The Case for Animal Rights*, Berkeley, University of California Press, 1983.

Rhees, R., ed.: see Wittgenstein.

Rolls, E. T., *The Brain and Emotion*, Oxford, Oxford University Press, 1999.

———, and Treves, A., *Neural Networks and Brain Function*, Oxford, Oxford University Press, 1998.

Rudwick, M. S., *Earth's Deep History: How It Was Discovered and Why It Matters*, Chicago, University of Chicago Press, 2014.

Runes, D., *The War against the Jew*, New York, Philosophical Library, 1968.

Sandberg, R., *Law and Religion*, Cambridge, Cambridge University Press, 2011.

Schmidt-Leukel, P., and Nehring, A., *Interreligious Comparisons in Religious Studies and Theology: Comparison Revisited*, London, Bloomsbury, 2016.

Sharma, A., ed., *God, Truth and Reality: Essays in Honour of John Hick*, London, Macmillan, 1993.

Shavit, U., 'Can Muslims Befriend Non-Muslims? Debating *al-wala' wa-al-bara'* (Loyalty and Disavowal) in Theory and Practice', *Islam and Christian-Muslim Relations*, November 2013, pp. 1–22.

Shaw, J., 'The Moral Imagination and a Sense of God', in Lemcio, *qv*, pp. 113–27.

Silberstein, L. J., *Jewish Fundamentalism in Comparative Perspective: Religion, Ideology, and the Crisis of Modernity*, New York, New York University Press, 1993.

Skya, W., *Japan's Holy War: The Ideology of Radical Shinto Ultranationalism*, Durham, Duke University Press, 2009.

Smith, B. K., *Classifying the Universe: The Ancient Indian Varna System and the Origins of Caste*, Oxford, Oxford University Press, 1994.

Suleiman, S. R., and Crosman, I., *The Reader in the Text: Essays on Audience and Interpretation*, New York, Columbia University Press, 1983.

Tablet: see 'Following Peter?'.

Tee, C., *The Gülen Movement in Turkey: The Politics of Islam and Modernity*, London, I. B. Tauris, 2015.

Thoreau, H. D., *Walden* (1854), New York, The New American Library, 1960.

Tinbergen, N., 'On Aims and Methods of Ethology', *Zeitschrift für Tierpsychologie*, 20, 1963, pp. 410–33.

Towards a Global Ethic: see Beversluis.

'Trojan Horse: The Real Story . . .', *Guardian*, 'Long Read', September 2001, p. 1.

Tuchman, B., *The March of Folly: From Troy to Vietnam*, London, The Folio Society, 1997.

Volf, M., *Exclusion and Embrace: A Theological Exploration of Identity, Otherness, and Reconciliation*, Nashville, Abingdon Press, 1996.

Vulliamy, E., 'Bridging the Gap', *The Guardian*, 13 July 2008.

Ward, W., *The Life of John Henry Cardinal Newman*, vol. II, London, Longmans, 1912.

Waugh, E., *Sword of Honour*, London, Folio Society, 1990.

Whitman, W., 'Song of Myself' in *Leaves of Grass*, London, Nonesuch, 1964.

Williams, M., and Penman, D., *Mindfulness: A Practical Guide to Finding Peace in a Frantic World*, London, Piatkus, 2011.

Williams, P., *Mahayana Buddhism: The Doctrinal Foundations*, London, Routledge, 1991.

Williams, R. E., *A Century of Punch*, London, Heinemann, 1956.

Wilson, D. S., *Does Altruism Exist? Culture, Genes, and the Welfare of Others*, New Haven, Yale University Press, 2015.

Wittgenstein, L., *Preliminary Studies for the 'Philosophical Investigations', Generally Known as the Blue and Brown Books*, Oxford, Blackwell, 1950.

——, *Philosophical Investigations*, Oxford, Blackwell, 1953.

Wolff, J., *Narrative of a Mission to Bokhara in the Years 1843–1845 to Ascertain the Fate of Colonel Stoddart and Captain Conolly*, New York, Harper & Brothers, 1845.

Copyright acknowledgements

The publisher and author acknowledge with thanks permission to reproduce extracts from the following:

Additional text 2 is based on my chapter, 'Christianity and Non-Christian Religions: A Neo-Darwinian Revolution?' in Sharma, pp. 87–97 (for details see Bibliography).

Additional text 3 draws on part of the Introduction to *The Message and the Book: Sacred Texts of the World's Religions*, pp. 1–5, 14–16. I am grateful to the publishers in each case, Palgrave Macmillan for the first, and Atlantic Books for the second, for permission to use this material.

The extract from 'Sudden Heaven' from *Collected Poems by Ruth Pitter*, copyright © Enitharmon Press 1996, is reproduced by kind permission. <www.enitharmon. co.uk>

Every effort has been made to seek permission to use copyright material reproduced in this book. The publisher apologizes for those cases where permission might not have been sought and, if notified, will formally seek permission at the earliest opportunity.

Index

Index

Index

Index

Index

Index

Index

Index

Rohingya 7, 40

Rolls, E. T. 66, 174

Roosevelt, Eleanor 62

Rudwick, M. S. 32, 34

rules 3, 14, 22, 31, 40, 45, 63, 76, 101, 102, 159

Runes, D. 40, 138

sacred space 98

sacred texts 89, 153, 155–63

sacred, the, and the profane 140, 154

sacrifice 48, 50, 51, 138

St Paul's Cathedral 16

Salafi 36, 41, 42, 87, 89, 102, 172

salvation 18, 77, 90, 111, 112, 141, 143, 144, 145, 146, 147, 148

Samaritans 106

satya-yuga 89

Saudi Arabia 61

sciences 21, 25, 31, 32, 33, 34, 35, 36, 37, 91, 114, 115, 134, 149

scientism 33

Scientology 16

Scripture 58, 103, 141, 166, 170

second level of phenomenology 30, 48, 85, 105

secularism 33, 36, 37, 70

selection 45, 46, 47, 48, 49, 149

self 46, 47, 49, 55, 65, 71, 75, 80, 83, 84, 93, 96, 101, 135, 145

'selfish gene' metaphor 45, 46, 47, 48; as false 46, 48, 81

selfless gene 46, 65

Seneca 140

sex 45, 54, 76, 89

Shapiro, S. 63

Sharia 4, 40, 60, 61, 126, 127, 128

sharing 38, 74, 76, 77, 90, 91, 97, 104, 108, 109, 114, 121, 158, 161

Sharma, A. 135

Shavit, U. 41

Shaw, J. 121

shukyo 19

Shylock 39, 53, 55, 66, 69

Sikhs 107, 129

sin/fault 50, 57, 61, 144, 145, 151

Skya, W. 91

SMEALCS 117

Smith, B. K. 57

social behaviour 19

social context/life 30, 37, 38, 42, 44, 54, 58, 65, 84, 100, 114

social division 129

social organization 8, 21, 44, 56, 74, 84, 89, 96

social studies 154, 160

society/societies 1, 5, 30, 35, 38, 43, 47, 49, 56, 57, 58, 62, 67, 74, 75, 76, 77, 90, 91, 92, 97, 101, 103, 104, 106, 121, 127, 128, 129, 130, 131, 151, 156

sociolinguistics 74

sociologists 90, 99

sociology 23, 30

Index